# The Endpoint Security Paradox

## 2nd Edition

**Andrew Avanessian**

**THE ENDPOINT SECURITY PARADOX**
**REALISING IMPLEMENTATION SUCCESS**

## Credits

**Author:** Andrew Avanessian

**Reviewers:** James Maude, Senior Security Engineer & Laura Butler, Head of Content

**Contributors:**

Paul Davies, Senior Technology Consultant,

Paul specialises in assisting clients in the Consultancy, Financial Services, Retail and Telecommunications sectors, to implement technical controls to meet a broad range of governance, risk and compliance objectives. His experience spans 15 years both as a vendor and implementor in the GRC arena, with a strong focus on information security.

Laura Butler, Head of Content

With almost ten years' experience in the technology sector, Laura is a CIM qualified professional who specialises in B2B content, communications and brand strategy. With an expansive knowledge of the cybersecurity space and keen eye for content, Laura was an important contributor to this book.

**Cover Design:** Jonathan Clarke

**Thanks to all who have made this version possible.**

**Dedicated to Simon Avanessian** who taught me three things; 1) Never give up 2) Always do the difficult things first 3) Anything can be achieved with hard work.

## About the Author

Andrew established the consultancy and technology services at a global endpoint security company Avecto. He regularly provides security and technology advice to large enterprises, overseeing software deployments across millions of endpoints. His background in IT infrastructure ensures he can clearly translate complex requirements, finding technical solutions to commercial challenges. With a keen interest in cybersecurity and the end user experience, Andrew is a regular contributor to press articles and has spoken at numerous security and technology events. He has also appeared on the BBC and CNBC News channels.

Andrew holds an Honours degree in Computer Science, together with a number of industry recognised qualifications from Microsoft, Apple and CompTIA. These include Microsoft MCP, MCSA, MCSE, ITIL.

# Endorsements

"The biggest rule in Endpoint Security is that there is no security unless you remove end user admin rights and follow the principle of least privilege. Many people tend to think that this cannot be achieved without compromising usability or productivity - this is not the case. In this book, Andrew Avanessian explains how to successfully guide a project to achieve the highest security, while still keeping end users happy and productive. Remember that getting rid of excessive rights is not just about security, but it can help you take down the amount of support tickets in your company and keep your armada of endpoints serving their users longer and better!"

**— Sami Laiho, Microsoft MVP and Ethical Hacker**

"The Endpoint Security Paradox is a masterful analysis of the productivity/security puzzle, providing a simple and effective solution in the process."

**— Eric Cole, CEO of Secure Anchor Consulting**

"A must-read for every security professional. Avanessian lays out both a compelling and incredibly effective solution to the conundrum of user productivity and endpoint security within every conceivable use case."

**— Kenneth Holley, CEO, Silent Quadrant**

# Preface

I've worked with thousands of clients, from SMBs to truly global enterprises, and one thing that constantly troubles me is that companies (large and small), never seem to truly understand WHY they are embarking on their latest security project. I have also seen many companies approach cybersecurity the hard way by trying to stop cyber attacks without having the proper foundations, meaning they are essentially starting at the wrong place. For example, around 90 per cent of critical vulnerabilities in Windows can be prevented simply by removing admin rights. However, I see people running with these rights all the time.

I am not saying the IT teams involved do not have any goals; of course, they do. However, it is often the case that they do not take a holistic view of their IT environment or projects, instead letting technology drive the objectives and not the business need. Businesses need to start with the end in mind, or in other words, the "why?" So before you start, ask yourself these questions:

1. Why are we running this project?
2. Do we really understand the requirements?
3. Have we asked the business owners what they need?
4. What benefit will we gain by doing this?

If you cannot honestly answer these questions, then you should go back to the drawing board, as ploughing ahead can result in poorly designed and implemented solutions. Putting this into context with my experiences in the IT security field, lack of answers has led to the "Swiss Cheese" effect – IT security systems full of holes! There are literally thousands of large enterprises that spend millions of dollars on IT security, and yet they are still breached.

IT security is not a dark art! You do not need the latest and greatest analysis tools or frameworks, and you do not even have to have a deep understanding of all the attack vectors that exist. You merely need to get the foundations right. Would you go out and leave your front door wide open or give your online banking details to all your acquaintances? No, you would not, yet I am often astounded at how many organisations do precisely this when it comes to IT security.

They get the basics wrong, and are breached, they throw money at the problem without fully understanding it and poorly implement the latest widget or appliance to hopefully "detect" the cybercriminals. Even the biggest firms do this - at the time of writing, a famous movie production company has just suffered a significant breach that could have been easily prevented by getting the security foundations right.

## Detection does not work, and yes, prevention is possible!

You will always, always, (yes, always) be two or more steps behind the cybercriminals. They do not have funding cycles; they do not operate change management windows. They spend all their time adapting their malware payloads. Detecting all of these threats is impossible!

However, if you analyse the significant headline breaches in the press today, I guarantee over 95 per cent could be prevented by getting the basics rights.

## So why am I writing this book?

I've spent years seeing IT projects fail and disaster after disaster play out in the media, so I'm writing this book to share my experiences in the IT security field to help improve organisational protection, specifically focusing on implementation success and best practices. I want to overcome some of the myths and cut through the noise to ensure businesses do not needlessly fall prey to attack.

 **95% of breaches could be prevented by getting the basics right.**

This book brings together my knowledge of deploying endpoint security (on both desktops and servers) to millions of endpoints across thousands of companies, including some of the largest on the planet. Therefore, I'll be focusing on solutions deployed directly onto the endpoint.

For me, the most significant issue facing endpoint security projects is the tradeoff between security and usability. Both ends of the spectrum are easy to achieve. However, getting the right balance between those seemingly polarised opposites is not.

The book is split into three parts. In part one, we will look at security principles and pitfalls. I am not going to detail specific threat vectors and techniques for analysing the attack chain, because there are hundreds of books out there doing that. However, I will provide a high-level overview of common attack vectors for completeness and context.

- Chapter 1 looks at the ever-changing threat landscape.
- Chapter 2 discusses vital security technologies to mitigate these attacks.
- Chapter 3 looks at the trade-offs between security and usability.
- Chapter 4 explores the pitfalls of common technology used to secure endpoints.

Part two looks at topics to help ensure the security foundations are laid correctly, in the context of a Defence in Depth strategy, whilst still enabling user freedom.

- Chapter 5 details proven technologies and techniques to combat attack.
- Chapter 6 takes a brief look at the costs and savings associated with Defence in Depth strategies.

Part three covers best practices for design, planning and implementation success. The implementation methodology discussed here has been tried and tested across hundreds of diverse organisations. We will examine the key challenges and considerations and help you build a plan for success.

- Chapter 7 focuses on implementation methodology.
- Chapter 8 looks at building group consensus to stop companies settling for average.
- Chapter 9 provides advice around vendor selection.

The principles discussed here apply generically to all successful projects, not just security. Naturally, every organisation has a unique set of challenges, but the desired result is common to all. Success!

There are many ways to achieve this, and this book will provide an implementation methodology that, is proven to be robust and secure in the most demanding of environments

# Contents

PART ONE

# Security Principles and Pitfalls

CHAPTER 1

# The ever-changing threat landscape

The news has often been dominated in recent years by headlines detailing the irrevocable damage caused by cybercrime and insider attacks. Cybercrime is now a trillion dollar industry and has an increasingly low barrier to entry. The amount of valuable data stored digitally has also skyrocketed, making the rewards on offer for cybercriminals huge. Unsurprisingly, it has attracted the attention of everyone from organised crime units to nation states looking to conduct cyber-espionage.

Every day we create 2.5 quintillion bytes of data, and by 2020, the amount of data stored will be 50 times larger than today[1]. In Q1 2018, McAfee recorded an average of five new threats every second[2], meaning the threat level and potential for damage to an organisation is astronomical.

---

1    http://www.testpoint.com.au/blog/by-2020-the-total-amount-of-data-stored-is-expected-to-be-50x-larger-than-today/)

2    https://www.mcafee.com/enterprise/en-us/assets/reports/rp-quarterly-threats-jun-2018.pdf

## 1.1. Top Security Breaches[3]

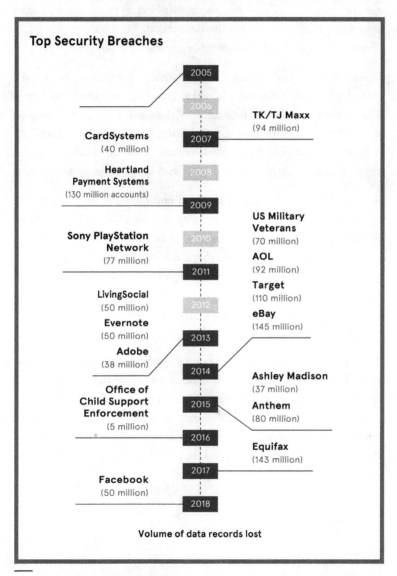

**Top Security Breaches**

2005

2006

**CardSystems**
(40 million)

2007

**TK/TJ Maxx**
(94 million)

**Heartland
Payment Systems**
(130 million accounts)

2008

2009

**US Military
Veterans**
(70 million)

**Sony PlayStation
Network**
(77 million)

2010

**AOL**
(92 million)

2011

**LivingSocial**
(50 million)

**Target**
(110 million)

2012

**Evernote**
(50 million)

**eBay**
(145 million)

2013

**Adobe**
(38 million)

2014

**Office of
Child Support
Enforcement**
(5 million)

**Ashley Madison**
(37 million)

2015

**Anthem**
(80 million)

2016

**Equifax**
(143 million)

2017

**Facebook**
(50 million)

2018

**Volume of data records lost**

3    http://www.informationisbeautiful.net/visualizations/worlds-biggest-data-breaches-hacks/
http://247wallst.com/technology-3/2016/04/15/2016-data-breaches-added-5-million-exposed-records-last-week/

The 2013 Target breach is a prime example of this. According to its earnings report, in the eight months following the attack, the retail chain's profits fell 62 per cent shareholders lost $148 million [4], and in a significant effort to reverse the destruction, $150 million was spent. The breach could have been avoided by getting the basics right.

Threats are not just coming from outside sources either. The scandal involving Edward Snowden - in which the computer expert and former CIA employee disclosed thousands of classified documents belonging to the NSA as a contractor for consulting firm Booz Allen Hamilton —-highlights the need for internal security as well as external. Again, these breaches could have been avoided with simple security principles.

So what does this all mean? There is so much hype in the cybersecurity space, with attack vector acronyms being discussed on a daily basis. More often than not, this serves to strike fear into the hearts of the average IT professional. We know that cybercrime inflicts pain on organisations and that as hacking methods become more sophisticated, the cybercrime economy is booming. However, beyond these certainties, there's significant confusion around what types of cybercrime exist and how to identify them.

There is no doubt that breaches exact a costly toll on victims, in terms of both time and money. These hidden costs often do not appear as line items on financial statements for a number of reasons. First, the costs are often indirect, being the result of wasted resources and missed opportunities. Second, organisations are incentivised to downplay the effects of cybercrime to avoid unwanted attention from the public and media.

4     http://qz.com/252466/target-customers-havent-forgiven-it-for-that-data-breach/

**The cost of data breaches due to malicious or criminal attacks increased from an average of $159 in 2014 to $170 per record in 2015. In 2014,, these attacks represented 42 per cent of root causes of a data breach, and this increased to 47 per cent of root causes in 2015[5]**

This price tag includes the costs incurred in detecting and responding to a breach, notifying victims, conducting post-response support, and lost business. Clearly, data breaches are financially burdensome on the organisations experiencing them.

In addition to these financial losses, organisations also suffer from lost time. Depending on the type of incident they experience, businesses may lose days, weeks, or even months of time to incident-response activities.

According to Accenture's 2017 Cost of Cyber Crime study, the average organisation spent $11.7 million on cyber crime costs in 2017, an increase of 23 per cent on the previous year[6].

In the following sections, I will take a look at some of the attack vectors to help put into context what we need to protect against.

5    2015 Cost of a Data Breach Study, IBM/The Ponemon Institute, May 2015
6    https://www.accenture.com/us-en/insight-cost-of-cybercrime-2017

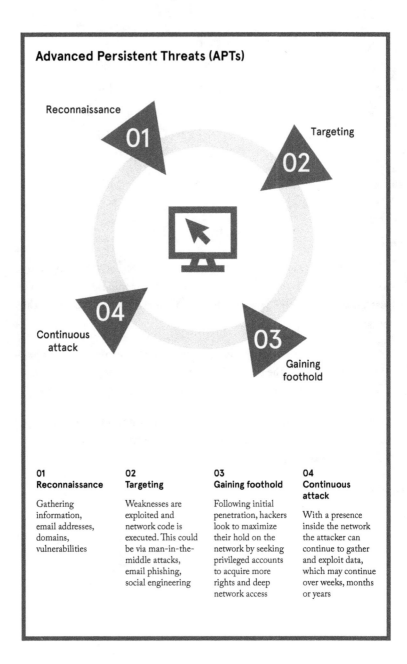

## Advanced Persistent Threats (APTs)

**01**
**Reconnaissance**

Gathering information, email addresses, domains, vulnerabilities

**02**
**Targeting**

Weaknesses are exploited and network code is executed. This could be via man-in-the-middle attacks, email phishing, social engineering

**03**
**Gaining foothold**

Following initial penetration, hackers look to maximize their hold on the network by seeking privileged accounts to acquire more rights and deep network access

**04**
**Continuous attack**

With a presence inside the network the attacker can continue to gather and exploit data, which may continue over weeks, months or years

## 1.2. Types of Attack

### 1.2.1.  Advanced Persistent Threats (APTs)

An APT is a sophisticated long-term threat launched against a specific target, with considerable technical capabilities and resources. Traditional security strategies are unable to fight against APTs, which can run over years and use multiple vectors. Crucially, attackers are organised and motivated.

In Ponemon's State of the Endpoint report, 65 per cent of respondents stated that APTs are frequently seen in their organisation's network -one of the most significant increases in noted threats[7].

### 1.2.2.  Targeted malware

Targeted malware is a type of malware destined for one specific organisation or industry. These are of particular concern because they are designed to capture sensitive information and are unique to the organisation. They utilise vectors such as spear phishing emails, vulnerable unpatched services or zero-day exploits — to name but a few — against line of business applications, such as Office.

### 1.2.3.  Phishing

Phishing is the process of sending malicious emails that appear to be legitimate, often spoofing email addresses from reputable organisations. Commonly they are trying to trick users into running malware, leaking sensitive information or performing financial transactions. According to McAfee, 97 per cent of users are unable to correctly identify phishing emails[8].

---

7    http://www.ponemon.org/blog/2015-state-of-the-endpoint-report-user-centric-risk
8    https://www.businesswire.com/news/home/20150512005245/en/97-People-Globally-
     Unable-Correctly-Identify-Phishing

### 1.2.4.  Zero-day attacks

Zero-day attacks mean that a previously unknown vulnerability is exploited before the vendor has released a patch. This is especially dangerous as research shows that 99.9 per cent of the exploited vulnerabilities had been compromised more than a year after the associated CVE was published[9].

Hackers are getting more sophisticated too. Verizon has noted multiple zero-day attacks, including an exploit in Hanscom's Hangul Word Processor by North Korean threat actors and the Microsoft Office Zero-Day CVE-2015-2424 leveraged by Tsar Team.

### 1.2.5.  Unpatched software

Unpatched software is classed as that which has vulnerabilities that have yet to be fixed by automatic updates. This can turn a zero-day threat into a forever day exploit if the relevant patch is not added.

F-Secure found that 70 per cent of businesses are leaving themselves vulnerable to attacks by failing to patch their software.

This is further compounded by End of Life (EOL) software such as Windows XP or older versions of Internet Explorer, which will no longer be patched by Microsoft. EOL software is often found running in corporate environments long after the vendor has stopped supporting it. This is mainly due to compatibility issues with Line of Business (LOB) applications, which were never designed to run with the latest versions and are too expensive to redevelop. These applications and their associated browser plugins pose a serious security concern.

### 1.2.6.  Insider threats

In addition to external cyber threats, organisations need to be aware of dangers from the inside, which can be even harder to protect against, as highlighted by the case of Edward Snowden.

---

9     http://www.verizonenterprise.com/uk/DBIR/2015/

Thales' 2018 Data Threat Report found that 51 per cent of companies in the US consider privileged users to be the most significant threat to their organisation, compared with 42 per cent who view cyber criminals as a serious risk[10].

When insider attacks are malicious, the individual is likely to be one step ahead of external threat actors because they already know what the company's assets are and how to gain access to them for theft, disclosure or destruction.

Meanwhile, according to Ponemon's Cost of Data Breach study, 27 per cent of data breaches are caused by human error, taking an average of 174 days to identify[11].

## 1.2.7.  Physical access

When we think of digital attacks, we often think of a hacker in a remote location. However, physical intrusions also happen, whether they originate from inside or outside an organisation.

Take a second to think about how often we open doors to strangers in our respective workspaces. We have no way of knowing their intent but we would consider it rude to ask them. There's nothing to say they are not carrying a USB stick containing malware that will bypass all network defences and be plugged directly into an endpoint.

It is a similar situation when dealing with employees. Organisations need to give staff enough access to documents to allow them to remain productive and prevent cases where they are continually having to ask for permissions. However, the more unrestricted access they provide, the more they leave themselves vulnerable.

10    https://www.thalesgroup.com/en/worldwide/security/press-release/2018-thales-data-
      threat-report-trends-encryption-and-data-security
11    http://www-03.ibm.com/security/data-breach/

### 1.2.8. **Exploit kits**

An interesting development in recent years is the introduction of exploit kits. These are toolkits that cybercriminals use to build malware attacks on the fly. Several kits have since been developed that can be sold or rented out like commercial products in underground markets.

A typical exploit kit usually provides a management console and preloaded vulnerabilities that make it easier for a cybercriminal to launch an attack. Exploit kits also provide graphical user interfaces, which typically include information on success rates and other types of statistics. Malware creation is now an industry in itself, with supportable software tools to help create new attacks. Worst of all, this will only get easier.

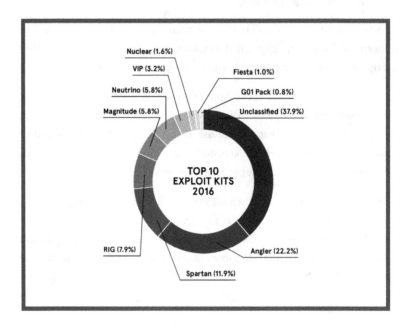

Nuclear (1.6%)
VIP (3.2%)
Neutrino (5.8%)
Magnitude (5.8%)
Fiesta (1.0%)
G01 Pack (0.8%)
Unclassified (37.9%)

TOP 10
EXPLOIT KITS
2016

RIG (7.9%)
Spartan (11.9%)
Angler (22.2%)

# 1.3. Social engineering

Malware and social engineering use essentially the same tactics; exploit someone or something, remain undetected and gain access. In 1995 Kevin Mitnik was arrested for penetrating some of the most well-guarded systems in the world, including the likes of Sun Microsystems, Digital Equipment Corporation, Motorola, Netcom, and Nokia. So what was the weapon of choice for the FBI's most wanted hacker? Social engineering. Kevin had learned at an early age that people were a great resource and could be manipulated for information and access.

Fast forward 20 years and what have we learnt? Surprisingly little. The aircraft part manufacturer FACC was recently tricked into transferring over $50 million to a Chinese Agricultural Bank; Amazon has been socially engineered into giving away customers' personal details. Belgian Bank Crelan lost $75.8 million to a fake CEO. Overall, the FBI attributed $1.2 billion of losses globally to social engineering fraud between 2014 and 2016[12].

Ultimately, the best security in the world can be bypassed with social engineering, because the user is the weakest link in the chain. In IT we often create heroes, all-powerful beings, omnipresent on the network with power over the life and death of data and running processes.

In reality, they are human, they are fallible, and therefore they can still fall into the same social engineering traps as anyone else. There's just something about the digital world that renders many blind.

For instance, in a bank, we do not give the branch manager keys to the building and the code for the vault, then leave him to it. There is an audit; time released locks and clearly defined access procedures.

---

12    http://www.ft.com/cms/s/0/83b4e9be-db16-11e5-a72f-1e7744c66818.
      html#axzz46NaYmanF

This prevents attackers from easily engineering their way in. Maybe they can dress as an "IT guy" and get behind the counter, but the multiple layers of defence should stop them getting to the vault.

However, when it comes to our wealth of digital data and IP (Intellectual Property), we often have people at junior levels holding the key to the vault, with varying degrees of accountability.

Organisations are not always switched on to this, but physical and digital defences need to work together. A denial-of-service (DoS) attack is often used to distract from financial fraud or data breaches. Ransomware and malware can trick or pressure users into revealing passwords or financial information. Often, employees assume that social engineering is limited to emails asking for monetary donations, such as those from Nigerian royalty, and can easily be avoided. However, even Nigerian phishing emails are more sophisticated than they appear, serving as an efficient way to target "Mugu" (fools).

In digital we talk about defence in depth (DiD) but rarely do we implement this for people. To break into an organisation from a computer, we might need to bypass firewalls, avoid Intrusion Detection Systems, find a vulnerable machine, create an exploit, avert detection, pivot and move laterally to reach the target endpoint. Far from a trivial task. To socially engineer our way in we might simply have to ask the target user to "have a look at this invoice", "click this link" or simply call them up and say "Mark from accounts needs to know X".

## 1.4. Summary: Let's get proactive

Reactive security strategies alone are no longer enough to overcome today's next-generation threats. Cybercriminals are always evolving their tactics and approaches, making it impossible to detect a new threat - even those that have only slightly been modified. When decoded, we can see that today's cybercriminals are often using old techniques and approaches, which have been altered and sewn together with new attacks.

With more and more attacks taking place, traditional security measures, such as antivirus, monitoring/session recording and passwords are not enough when used in isolation. These legacy detection approaches just do not work! You will always be two to three steps behind the cybercriminals. However, by layering multiple strategies, it is possible to create a balanced security architecture.

Attitudes towards security also need to be changed. Fundamentally, security is a culture that everyone has to buy into, and we should not differentiate between the endpoint and the employee, as good security principles still apply. Without these in place, we leave gaps that can be socially engineered and exploited.

Time and time again I see security vendors offering the latest widget or system that is going to "save the world". However, there is no silver bullet when it comes to overcoming cyber challenges. Securing your systems against the latest attacks is not rocket science. Likewise, when people talk about stopping the cybercriminals getting inside, it is simply not enough. Ensuring you have perimeter defences is essential, but the traditional eggshell approach to security (where the outsides are hard, but the insides are soft) is not enough and also stuck in the 1990s – more on this later.

Yes, there are always new zero day exploits uncovered, but I will be explaining how the right security foundations can thwart these attacks. I will also be sharing industry expert advice, which backs up these techniques.

Remember where your data is stored! Your organisation's IP is on the endpoint, whether that be a desktop or server. The weakest link is your end users, and these will be targeted.

# CHAPTER 2

# Security foundations

In this chapter, we will take a look at four key security principles that form the foundations of any successful security model. When linked together, these form the basis of a defence in depth strategy. They are proven to mitigate around 90 per cent of Windows vulnerabilities and 85 per cent of targeted attacks. I will also cross-reference advice provided by organisations such as CIS, GCHQ, The Australian Signals Directive and many more. We will look into how to implement them in chapters 4 and 5.

## 2.1. The four key foundations of strong security
• • • • • • • • • • • • • • • • • • • • • • • • • • • • • • • • • • • • • • • • • • • • •

### 2.1.1 Least privilege security – the best place to start

Least privilege security is the practice of assigning users and programs the least permissions required to complete a given task.

The Department of Defense Trusted Computer System Evaluation Criteria, (DOD-5200.28-STD), also known as the Orange Book, defines least privilege as a principle that "requires that each subject in a system be granted the most restrictive set of privileges (or lowest clearance) needed for the performance of authorised tasks. The application of this principle limits the damage that can result from accident, error or unauthorised use."[13]

Least privilege was first put forward as a design principle by Jerry Saltzer and Mike Schroeder over 30 years ago. According to Saltzer and Schroeder:

"Every program and every user of the system should operate using the least set of privileges necessary to complete the job. Primarily, this principle limits the damage that can result from an accident or error. It also reduces the number of potential interactions among privileged programs to the minimum for correct operation, so that unintentional, unwanted, or improper uses of privilege are less likely to occur.

"Thus, if a question arises related to misuse of a privilege, the number of programs that must be audited is minimised. Put another way, if a mechanism can provide 'firewalls', the principle of least privilege provides a rationale for where to install the firewalls. The military security rule of 'need-to-know' is an example of this principle."[14]

## Reduce the number of users with excessive privileges – AKA least privilege

Now the textbook definition is out of the way, we can put this into practical terms. In other words, if your job function involves checking emails, surfing the internet, and running standard applications, then your user account should not be granted administrative rights to your endpoint.

---

13    Department of Defense Trusted Computer System Evaluation Criteria (Orange Book) at http://zedz.net/rainbow/5200.28-STD.html.

14    Department of Defense Trusted Computer System Evaluation Criteria (Orange Book) at http://zedz.net/rainbow/5200.28-STD.html.

Removing administrative privileges from end users is a vital step in improving security by ensuring that endpoints cannot easily be compromised. Preventing unknown processes from running with administrative privileges limits the damage that can be done should an endpoint be compromised by malware, as well as reducing the risk of data loss, misconfiguration and insider threats.

## Endpoint least privilege is not rocket science

Least privilege security may sound complicated, but in reality, it is simple . Privileges can be assigned to user accounts through the built-in security groups, providing system administrators with an easy way to restrict privileges for the majority of users. While this is not perfect, it is a reasonable trade-off between security and usability.

Although this book focuses on the activities at the endpoint and its security, it is essential to also consider the broader principle of least privilege and think about how this applies to data access, databases and all aspects of digital and physical security.

**Here are my top tips:**

- Get the basics right and do not use shared accounts – make sure that your employees and customers are uniquely identified
- Minimise or eliminate all guest and anonymous accounts
- Verify your password policy for best practices regarding complexity, length, and expiration. Make sure that your service account passwords meet these requirements as well
- Use two-factor authentication where possible

> • Privileges should be based on a user's needs, rather than a standard template. Generally, this is done with physical security, but we often fail to apply the same principles in the digital world

## 2.2. Application control (AKA whitelisting)

Removing administrative accounts goes a long way to securing user accounts and protecting critical parts of the system from accidental or malicious change. If you have done these things, you should be pleased with yourself (and proud). Even if administrator accounts are removed, the user and the system are still exposed to applications and malware that can execute from the user's profile, such as portable apps, as well as vulnerabilities in trusted line of business applications.

Application whitelisting provides a higher level of control over the software environment. Downloading and running unapproved software is one of the most common ways that devices are compromised. Whereas detection technologies laboriously scan the endpoint looking for known bad files, behaviours,malicious content and threats, whitelisting takes a very different approach and blocks everything except those applications and behaviours known to be trusted.

There are thousands of applications and malware programs that will run in the context of a standard user. This is often overlooked by organisations who think removing admin rights will be good enough. There have been multiple high-profile breaches that did not require administrator privileges, hence the need to prevent unknown code from executing.

Application whitelisting is rated as 'essential' by industry bodies such as CIS, as well as compliance mandates like GCHQ, and NIST, making it crucial for preventing malware.

Therefore, we need to configure the build to only allow the execution of trusted applications and block the execution of the unknown. This is achieved with a whitelist, and it is crucially important, as modern modular APT attacks use a myriad of techniques to drop payloads in their attempts to exploit a zero-day attack. I have included an example attack chain, using genuine vulnerabilities, below:

1. The user is socially engineered to click a link to an attacker-controlled website

2. HTML/JS launcher page serves Flash exploit

3. Flash exploit triggers CVE-2015-3043, executing shellcode

4. Shellcode downloads and runs executable payload (app control would have prevented)

5. Executable payload exploits local privilege escalation (CVE-2015-1701) to steal System token

A whitelist is a set of programs, scripts, or processes that are trusted and therefore approved to run. It is a good practice to create a whitelist of permitted applications, rather than blocking banned programs using a blacklist. It is impossible to include every malicious application in a blacklist, so it is preferable to attempt to define what is allowed in a whitelist.

Typically, whitelists have been challenging to create and maintain. However, basing the list on trusted locations rather than individual applications ensures the list is easy to manage. This allows for the effective control of applications by adding known and trusted locations and sources to whitelists, while unknown and untrusted apps are prevented from executing actions that can threaten the system.

At this point, it is worth reiterating that this approach will only work if you have removed administrator accounts. Otherwise, these rules can be circumvented.

### 2.1.3.  Use of standard, secure system configurations

Manufacturers and resellers often ship operating systems and devices with default configurations aimed at ease-of-deployment and ease-of-use, not security. Basic controls, open services and ports, default accounts or passwords, older (vulnerable) protocols, pre-installation of unneeded software - all of these can be exploitable in their default state.

To prevent attackers from exploiting vulnerable services and settings, establish, implement, and actively manage (including tracking, reporting on, and correcting) the security configuration of laptops, servers, and workstations using rigorous configuration management and change control processes. Once again, bodies such as CIS, GCHQ, CESG, NIST and CPNI recognise this as a fundamental step in securing your environment.

Failure to manage the proper configuration of your endpoints can lead to a wide variety of security problems. If every system has a standardised configuration, which is known to be secure, managing these systems and protecting them will be far easier.

Define and apply a secure baseline configuration to all devices, and ensure they are updated with the necessary security patches. Guaranteeing the configuration is continually managed will avoid a security "decay" as new vulnerabilities are reported. If not, attackers will find opportunities to exploit both network-accessible services and client software.

Once again, moving administrator privileges plays a big part in ensuring configurations stay standard and current. If users have administrator privileges, they can fundamentally change any setting they like.

## 2.1.4. Patch application and system software

Unpatched operating systems and applications are vulnerable to attack. It is vitally important that the operating system and line of business applications be kept up to date with the latest patches and hotfixes. By applying patches quickly and keeping them up to date, you close the door to malware and hackers looking to exploit flaws. CIS, GCHQ, CESG, NIST, ADoD and CPNI all recognise patching a critical cyber defence.

As I mentioned earlier, one statistic that puts this into context is that 99.9 per cent of vulnerabilities were compromised a year after CVE publication![15] Typically, there is a 120 day lead time between a patch/ update being released and it being deployed within the enterprise. This is a massive window of opportunity for the cybercriminals.

Operating system hotfixes and updates can be managed in a number of ways. The technology exists to proactively scan for vulnerabilities and address any known flaws to reduce the risk of systems being compromised. Two common options are; 1) Microsoft's Windows Server Update Services (WSUS) and 2) System Centre Configuration Manager (SCCM).

Modern operating systems come preloaded with many tools and services that would have previously required installation and management. For example, early operating systems needed USB drivers and productivity applications such as PDF readers installing and maintaining. Keeping your OS and any of these apps updated reduces not only risk, but also the cost of ownership.

Third-party applications often have automated patching mechanisms, but some require users to manually install updates and provide consent using an administrative account, forcing IT to choose between removing administrative accounts and allowing users to update applications as needed.

---

15    http://www.verizonenterprise.com/uk/DBIR/2015/

Many thirdparties provide Software as a Service (SaaS) offerings that make patch management more manageable by providing support for Microsoft patches and mainstream applications and OSs such as Adobe, Linux and Java. However, there is no perfect solution, and many come with their own trade-offs.

Many thirdparties provide Software as a Service (SaaS) offerings that make patch management more manageable by providing support for Microsoft patches and mainstream applications and OSs such as Adobe, Linux and Java. However, there is no perfect solution, and many come with their own trade-offs.

## 2.3. Defence in depth still works – don't just take my word for it

Defence in depth (DiD) is a term coined for a proven military strategy where multiple defences frustrate the enemy and prevent the attack. In the event that one of the security layers is compromised, other layers still provide the necessary protection for the system. Evidence has shown that to combat increasingly sophisticated threats, a layered approach that prioritises high impact and proactive solutions are the best defence.

The four security foundations discussed in the previous section are recommendations of key industry bodies, and when applied together, they offer a substantiated framework for building your DiD strategy.

The Centre for Internet Security (CIS) states in its 'Critical Security Controls for Effective Cyber Defence' report that a cyber defence system must be based around several "critical tenets" that create a DiD approach. The top five recommendations of its 20 Critical Controls, named as "five quick wins", echo findings from the Australian DoD and the UK government, which have also propounded the benefits of a DiD strategy.

By placing the above four strategies at the heart of DiD, it is possible to create a balanced, layered approach. Other bodies such as CESG, GCHQ, NISTand CPNI echo the above methods.

Tests have shown these security controls,when implemented together, mitigate 85 per cent of targeted cyber attacks. These recommendations are based on the Australian Skills Directorate's analysis of reported security incidents and vulnerabilities detected by ASD in testing the security of Australian government networks.[16]

The removal of administrative rights alone - as recommended by GCHQ (CESG) - mitigates 85 per cent of targeted attacks and 80 per cent of Critical Microsoft vulnerabilities.[17]

16    http://www.asd.gov.au/infosec/mitigationstrategies.htm
17    Microsoft Vulnerabilities Report 2015 http://learn.avecto.com/2015-microsoft-vulnerabilities-report

## 2.4. **Summary: A word of caution – there is no silver bullet!**

When it comes to cyber security, there is no silver bullet! A layered strategy, combining proactive and reactive measures is needed to track, trap and overcome modern cyber attacks properly.

As discussed, applying the four strategies mitigates 85% of targeted attacks. These strategies must be implemented thoroughly across 100 per cent of your endpoints (desktops and servers). It only takes one user running with an admin account to be the launch pad into your network.

Get the basic foundations right, and the rest becomes much easier.

In the following chapters, we will look at how we can implement technologies to achieve the above.

CHAPTER 3

# Good advice is hard to follow

To this day, Microsoft Windows does not provide a comprehensive solution for the problem of balancing security with user freedom. There are many potential workarounds that organisations have attempted, but historically they have not been appropriately utilised, or they consume too much resource while leaving the organisation open. This ultimately leads to a failed solution.

Having read the previous chapters, you may be thinking "I know all this", and if you are, that is a good start. However, ask yourself if you are 100 per cent certain you have applied these principles to 100 per cent of your environment? In my experience, most organisations have not, but the question is why? In this chapter, I will explore why organisations often fail to follow the above advice.

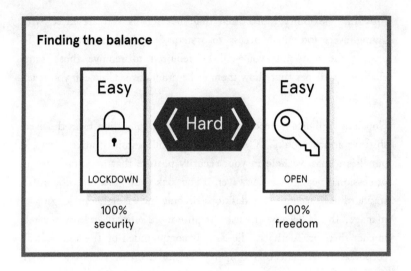

## 3.1. **100% security or 100% freedom? That is the question**

All organisations are faced with a seemingly impossible compromise: your users require flexibility to do their jobs, as well as protection from external and internal attackers and the knowledge that they have a compliant environment in which to work.

 100 per cent freedom is easy! Being 100 per cent secure is easy if you are happy that your users cannot do anything! Liken it to encasing your endpoints in a concrete box - yes they are secure, but the user experience is non-existent!

Providing flexibility more often than not means you are faced with giving users too much access to systems, applications and data. To protect the endpoint, you will be required to remove those same elevated privileges that allow them to be productive. How can you reach a compromise?

Constant vigilance is needed to protect your organisation from the ever-shifting attack vectors. If you grant users full administrative access, it punches a massive hole in your security posture that is tantamount to professional negligence. However, if you lock your workforce down to a standard user account, the desktops become increasingly challenging to manage. This is because the users require more support and you severely impact their productivity. The issue is compounded by the fact that all corporate IP (Intellectual Property) is stored on or accessed through the endpoint.

 **Giving users 100% freedom is easy, give them administrative rights and allow them to do what they want, where they want and how they want! They are free but your secure posture is none existent!**

Either approach has its downsides, and both come with increased costs and risks. The goal should be providing the right set of privileges and security to meet your organisational and user roles and requirements.

Companies will struggle to balance security with user productivity, especially with the ever increasing tech-savviness of Gen Y employees, who expect the same freedoms in work that they have outside of it.

## 3.2. Why is 100% freedom a challenge?

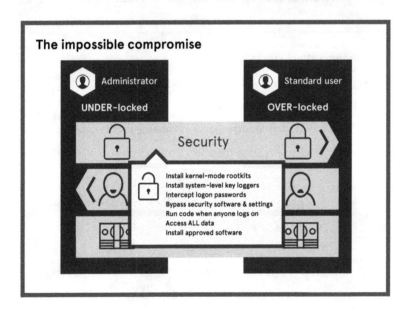

Managing an IT environment is a tough job. The board expects the IT department to keep the company's data safe from hackers and unauthorised access, whilst users and middle management often have other ideas about what constitutes a good security, preferring to circumvent policies or have themselves exempted, without a valid business reason. Sometimes, however, complaints about security are justified due to poor design or execution.

The administrator account provides an open and flawed security stance; users and malware potentially have complete access to the system. It is often considered that a single machine running with administrative account is not a risk to other devices connected to the same network. However, this is not the case. If one device becomes infected with malware, it can pivot the network to launch attacks against other devices, including servers and network hardware. At worst this will impede system performance or bring entire networks to a halt.

> **Common attacks include:**
> - Scanning the network for vulnerabilities
> - Exploiting pass the hash attacks
> - Credential theft for other services running on the network

 An admin account is like a bucket full of holes. Essentially you can install anything, change any settings, access any data, disable/bypass any security system, one way or another!

In a survey conducted by Ponemon Research, 55 per cent[18] of IT professionals admitted to having no visibility of employee behaviour, application access and software downloads, while 40 per cent said the percentage of users with administrative accounts is increasing year-on-

---

18    https://www.avecto.com/news-and-events/press-releases/study-finds-52-percent-of-enterprises-defenseless-against-cyber-attacks

year. This is creating a significant security vulnerability, yet organisations are often not aware of how to solve this issue.

If security gets in the way of a user's ability to do his or her job, then it will be weakened or disabled. While such actions may be acceptable as part of the troubleshooting process, configuration changes frequently remain permanent.

Administrative accounts are often seen as a status symbol to users, especially IT and senior management, so they may be reluctant to give them up. If endpoint security is not implemented correctly and users efficiently educated, it will most likely start a mutiny!

# 3.3. Why is 100% security a challenge?

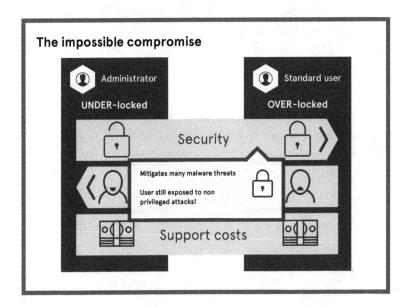

On the other side, the standard user account is the most secure account Microsoft can provide and mitigates the risk of 80 per cent of the critical security vulnerabilities identified. Over the past five years, the number of vulnerabilities has risen by 111 per cent.[19]

 Even back in 2011, Gartner analyst Neil MacDonald stated that removing administrative rights is "the single most important way to improve endpoint security. Common sense is not always common practice." [20]

Initially it may look like the standard user account has all the answers to our problems, but unfortunately, it does not. The account is still exposed to user data level attacks, such as "ransomware" based exploits. There is a whole host of malware that can run in the context of the standard user and compromise data within their profile. The malware's aim is twofold; 1) access and steal as much data as possible, and 2) proliferate across the network to find a system running with an administrative account, to embed deeper and cause further damage.

In the example of CryptoLocker, malware infected 600,000 systems and earned its creators more than $1 million, with the aim of encrypting all data the user has access to, including network shares. Its payloads can be delivered by a wide range of attack sources - websites, documents and fake updates.

---

19    Avecto vulnerabilities report – see avecto website
20    http://blogs.gartner.com/neil_macdonald/2011/08/23/the-single-most-important-way-to-improve-endpoint-security/

## Why are administrative accounts tolerated?

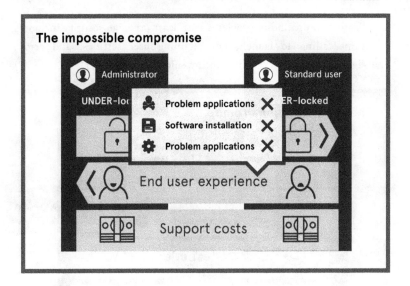

Just removing administrative accounts from all users creates challenges in its own right. If a user does not have access to an administrator account, there are hundreds of operating system functions and thousands of applications that will just not run. The situation is made worse by the fact that IT departments have traditionally relied on users to install approved software and fix problems as directed by the help desk or without any instruction at all. This requires that users have administrative access to systems.

This self-service approach is standard, especially in small and medium-sized enterprises, where support staff may not have the necessary skills to help users who do not have administrative access to their endpoints.

One huge problem you will run into is application compatibility, which is often caused by developers assuming end users will be logging on with administrator privileges. This results in software that requires administrative accounts to work correctly.

Application compatibility problems with least privilege security include; programs failing to launch, not retaining user settings, and error messages appearing, all of which inconvenience the end user.

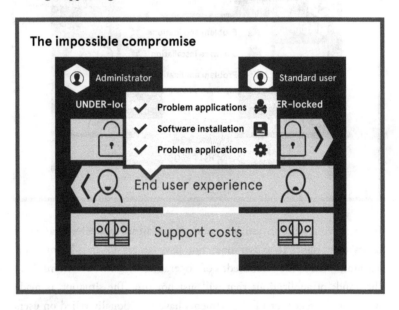

As we have seen, the alternative is that users are given an administrative account which then allows them to install any application, run any application and change any setting. This is simply too much power and can lead to issues created by the user. Also, malware will run in the context of the logged-in user and will have access to the same resources as the user.

Users will often reject least privilege accounts, insisting that "I will be careful" or "I know what I am doing". Again, this often comes back to an admin account being a status symbol. The basis for this rejection is often centred around usability. When users undertake risky activities, such as browsing the internet (computer expert or not), it is impossible to be sure that malevolent software will not be accidentally launched through malicious code embedded in web pages.

These are designed to launch silently without the user's knowledge or exploit an unpatched vulnerability in the operating system. Users are the weakest link, increasingly being targeted by attackers. Recent examples include targeted attacks which prey on the personal assistants of the C-level, to garner information used to find routes into an organisation.

This is not just a desktop problem. All of the same challenges apply to servers. Least privilege security needs to be applied to servers as a matter of course, as the benefits that least privilege brings to servers is more important than on desktops. This is because of the diversity of the services being provided by servers, with potentially thousands of users affected if a server is down.

In short, implementing least privilege on a Windows operating system stifles the user experience. Unless the people in your environment are classic task-based workers, doing the same job every day (i.e. call centre staff, Point of Sale terminals), you will struggle to make this work.

## Non-administrative installations

It is becoming common for software to be packaged without the need for an administrative account to install. This creates the problem of unauthorised and unlicensed software being introduced. Alternatively, many applications are built in a portable format, meaning that no installation is required, and administrative rights are not needed to run the software. Users can copy the executable file to their endpoint and run the application.

Pertinent examples include Google Chrome, Firefox and other third party browsers. These make it possible to run applications not sanctioned in corporate environments. Even apps installed to the user's profile can introduce issues and result is data loss.

 **Research by Microsoft found that 57 per cent of workers install personal software on corporate machines.**

## 3.4. Supporting the end-user

To efficiently support end-user, in the least privilege environment, IT staff must have a detailed understanding of the following:

- **Windows security model:** Access control lists (ACLs), NT user rights, Integrity Levels, and User Account Control are all components of the security model. Many Windows support professionals have a limited understanding of these concepts.

- **Command line or PowerShell:** While GUI-based remote access tools can be useful, they are not always the most efficient way to gather data or run commands on remote computers, especially over slow network connections.

- **Automated software and patch installation:** Technologies such as Group Policy Software Installation, Windows Server Update Services (WSUS), System Centre Configuration Manager.

- **Management infrastructure:** Active Directory, Group Policy, System Centre Configuration Manager, cloud management systems and many more.

Without the proper infrastructure in place, IT staff will have to visit users' desktops, either physically or through remote access, far more often. The points listed above become crucial when supporting standard users.

Often IT professionals directly grant administrative accounts to users, as they do not understand how to work with these systems or just do not have the time or will to investigate the problem. As mentioned above, these rights are often left in place as it is an easy option to give people an admin account because they can't be bothered or do not know how to set the correct privileges to make things work.

## Remote support

Support tools such as Remote Desktop have been around for a long time and form a key part of the help desk's toolset. When users are running with standard user accounts, these tools are critical. The main reason for this is that you can no longer talk a user through a procedure over the phone if it requires administrative access (unless you create an administrative backdoor, although I would not advise it).

## Prepare for the worst

I can pretty much guarantee the standard method of connecting to the corporate network will break at some point, so provide at least one backup remote connection method. Also, be prepared for GUI-based remote access tools (i.e. Remote Desktop and Remote Assistance) to fail over slow network links. Therefore, it's important to have backup command line options in place using WS-Management and PowerShell. These command line tools can save the day and often speed up support. The downside is they require advanced knowledge.

## Remote and home-based workers

In my experience, remote workers are given administrative rights 95 per cent of the time. I often smile to myself when I go into an organisation, and I am told no one has administrative rights. I then ask how they support remote workers, only to find they, of course, get admin accounts. Remote workers bring with them a whole host of problems; greatest among them is that their devices need to stay up-to-date and distributing new software when required can be a nightmare.

## Supporting peripherals

It is important to establish what peripheral equipment your organisation will be supporting and how you will go about this. For example, you need to establish what equipment laptop users will be allowed to connect to their endpoints. Create a list of approved devices (such as printers, mobile phones etc.). A typical problem most IT teams have is laptop users' purchasing their own home office devices and expecting that support will be provided.

Standard users are limited as to what drivers they can install, which is often the root cause of support issues on peripherals. Standard users can install drivers if:

- The device driver is included in Windows out of the box
- IT has pre-staged in the local driver store (having a standardised list helps here)
- A driver is digitally signed according to the Windows Driver Signing Policy
- A driver is signed by a publisher that is already trusted by the local computer, and allow via Group Policy.

# 3.5. **Operating costs – you cannot win!**

Neither of the above scenarios minimise the costs of managing your endpoints. Indeed, both have the capacity to increase help desk calls.

With administrative accounts, the user may have created issues on the endpoint due to too much access by installing an incompatible application or changing a setting that has implications across your build beyond their knowledge. Imagine the impact of stopping critical system processes from an elevated Task Manager.

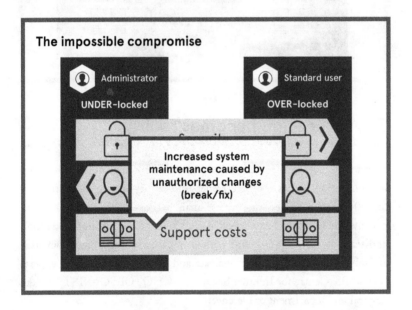

With standard accounts, users are so restricted that they need help performing even simple tasks and have to call the helpdesk to make the most minor of changes. This can mean a physical trip to the desktop in some cases, or it can mean a wait of up to six weeks if the app they need has to be packaged and deployed via existing application management systems and processes.

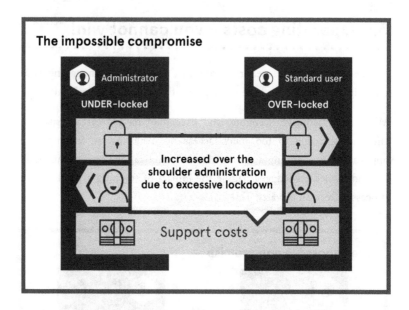

## 3.6. **Perception becomes reality**

Due to the complexities involved in the above compromises, there are misconceptions about the effectiveness of security strategies. In a survey of 500+ IT and IT security professionals by Ponemon[21], a hierarchy of perceived effectiveness was revealed. The table below highlights the tools and technologies organisations ranked in order of importance, which is entirely contradicted by the analysis and recommendations of experts such as the Centre for Internet Security, GCHQ, CESG, NIST, and the Australian Department of Defence.

---

21    http://www.ponemon.org/local/upload/file/Cyber%20Strategies%20for%20Endpoint%20
Defense%20Final1.pdf

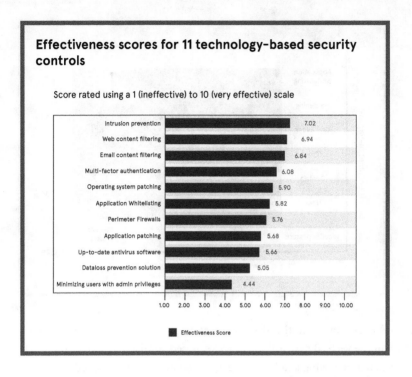

Looking at the above table, the top three technologies are essentially reactive "blacklisting" technologies based on detection. Reactive technologies simply do not work but are often implemented because they are understood and perceived to be easier to rollout. For example, if a "black box" can be implemented which magically stops the threats, this will be perceived as easier, especially if it does not touch the end user.

The same report found that 55% of IT professionals do not have visibility over their endpoints and as a result try to avoid implementing technology that touches the end user. However, this puts them at extreme risk.

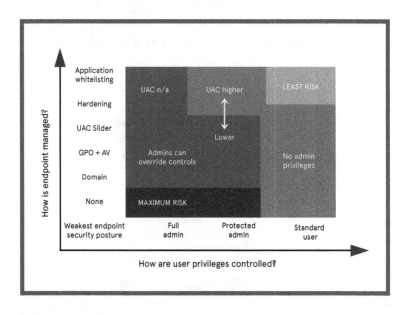

As you can see in this diagram, even implementing all the technologies up the vertical axis still leaves you exposed, whilst performing the single step of removing administrative rights takes you out of the red.

## 3.7. Summary: User experience is king

Navigating the polarised opposites of security and freedom is not easy; this is further compounded when IT departments are under pressure to bring new systems to market that will provide their organisations with a competitive edge.

So many times, I have seen security become an afterthought, rather than being an integral part of a design from the outset. Good security design is not always visible and thus not well understood by the c-suite, who pile on the pressure to release systems or improve user freedom.

Poorly implemented security will come to the forefront when, not if, a breach occurs. The pressure applied to release a system will quickly be forgotten about! To make matters worse, many IT professionals have a limited understanding of security. This lack of understanding often comes from the perception of security not being very "sexy", or worse, an unwanted headache.

There is a risk that endpoint security may reduce your ability to respond to ever-changing business needs. When least privilege security inhibits flexibility or the speed at which IT can respond, it will result in a failed project. So, where security is not an absolute necessity, it is regularly omitted for an easy life.

Securing IT systems to provide business continuity must be balanced with the ability to innovate. Organisations that move slowly will lose out to the competition, as IT systems play a key role in an organisation's agility. However, this is not an excuse for poor security design.

The above examples serve to demonstrate why the key security principles outlined in the previous chapters are not adopted in full.

 **Build security into a system from the outset, it should be part of your design requirements and not an after thought, that's the only way it will be a success.**

CHAPTER 4

# Why typical tools fall short

If it was not already, it is hopefully fast becoming clear that implementing these sound security principles and delivering basic cyber hygiene is not only worthwhile, it should be right at the top of your priority list.

There are several logical next questions from this realisation, including when, how, with which tool and with what budget you can achieve this. These last two are often seen as inextricably linked, and the latter can indeed be a challenge for organisations, perhaps because they do not have a dedicated IT security budget because funding has already been allocated.

What this often leads to is an organisation pursuing the "low-cost" (read: free) approach to the problem by using the native capabilities offered by the operating system and its supporting tools. It is worth remembering the adage says that "there is no such thing as a free lunch", and in this instance, the reality is often that the business still pays, it is just that the cost centre changes.

The question is, therefore, what capabilities are available natively and how feasible is it to implement these techniques using the native OS tools?

In this chapter, I will look at why organisations and IT professionals have been unable to balance freedom and security with the abundance of tech that exists today. In theory, it is probably achievable with a combination of all the tools below and an infinite amount of time. However, we live in the real world, and therefore I will explain what can be achieved and what issues you will come across with each approach.

The sections in this chapter align with the security foundations discussed in chapter 2. Therefore each of the technologies are grouped in their corresponding area. I'll be getting into quite a technical level of detail if this chapter, so feel free to skip ahead if any section aren't relevant to your role or business.

 This chapter focuses on Microsoft technologies due to their pervasiveness, broadly speaking the pros and cons discussed here apply to other vendors tooling. For good measure, I do include a section on macOS and mention other technologies where relevant.

## MICROSOFT WINDOWS

Microsoft has a long history of providing a range of tools and technologies to help organisations secure their endpoints, which they have continued to develop and refine over time.

In some cases, the technologies have been replaced, for example with Microsoft's Enhanced Mitigation Experience Toolkit, which saw many of it is features migrated into Windows 10. Other technologies, such as Microsoft's Application Control capabilities, have undergone several iterations, sometimes with a re-branding thrown in for good measure. Others have remained relatively unchanged through several generations of products.

Traditionally these technologies have not driven any revenue for Microsoft; they were provided to help customers, particularly large enterprises, meet compliance mandates and get more value from their investment. The cynics amongst you may conclude that Microsoft only developed these tools "just enough" to achieve these aims and I think that would probably be a fair assessment.

Now though, times have changed; Security is now a revenue stream and perhaps somewhat predictably, it has seen (and continues to see) more focus, investment and development from Microsoft as a result.

## 4.1. Least privilege – Endpoint Tools and Tech
· · · · · · · · · · · · · · · · · · · · · · · · · · · · · · · · · · · · · · · · · · · · · · · · · ·

This section discusses the technologies that provide least privilege capabilities.

# MICROSOFT – PRIVILEGE MANAGEMENT

Windows NT, released all the way back in 1993, introduced the ability to log into Windows with a defined set of system "privileges". In a Microsoft environment, a privilege describes the right of an account to perform specific system-related operations on a given computer. These privileges might include the ability to shut down the system, to change settings such as the system time, to perform a system backup, or to load drivers for a hardware device.

In conjunction with privileges, Windows environments also use permissions (commonly referred to as "access rights") to define a user's capabilities further. Whilst the assigned privileges control access to system resources and system-related activities, permissions are used to control access to "securable objects", which includes items like files, folders and registry keys.

**Definition:**

- **Privileges** differ from permissions in that they give users the ability to perform the system related operation, as shutting down the system.

- **Permissions** allow access to an object such as a registry key or a file.

User logon rights complete the trifecta of settings which define a user's capabilities, but these merely control whether a user may logon to a device locally, remotely, or as a service. It may also be used to deny the ability to perform those same tasks explicitly.

A system administrator may assign privileges and logon rights to accounts, whereas the system grants or denies access to a securable object based on the access rights granted in the Access Control Entries (ACEs) in an object's Discretionary Access Control List (DACL).

It is worth noting that whilst a permission may enforce a restrictive control upon a user, privileges assigned to that user may allow them to circumvent those controls. A simple example of this might be the SE_BACKUP privilege, commonly granted to allow full system backups to be performed (and restored), which necessitates the user being able to read and write files they would not ordinarily have access to read or modify.

# MICROSOFT PRIVILEGE MANAGEMENT – PRIVILEGED GROUPS AND USER RIGHTS ASSIGNMENTS

### What is this feature?

To simplify the configuration of both privileges and permissions, Windows includes a set of built-in groups with pre-assigned privileges and permissions, allowing users to be added to those groups (as part of rudimentary role-based management) and inherit their capabilities, rather than assigning them to individuals.

### What does this feature deliver?

In a default Windows installation, some groups exist by default, which is designed to allow users to perform specific management tasks on an endpoint. Two examples are:

**Backup Operators;** grants users rights to perform system-wide backups

**Network Operators;** grants users rights to manage network configuration settings

The default groups are:

- Administrators
- Backup Operators
- Cryptographic Operators
- Distributed COM Users
- Guests
- IIS_IUSRS
- Network Configuration Operators
- Performance Log Users
- Performance Monitor Users
- Power Users
- Remote Desktop Users
- Replicator
- Users
- Offer Remote Assistance Helpers

For a detailed description of the default local groups available in Windows platforms, and their associated default user rights, please see Appendix 1.

Whilst this wide range of groups exist, typically, the most commonly used built-in groups are 'Users' and 'Administrators'.

If you are assigned to the Administrators group, you can perform almost any task that is not specially protected by the operating system. Conversely, if you are assigned to the Users group, you can run installed programs and change settings that are not system-wide. However, you do not have the privileges to install software to the

Program Files directories or to modify protected areas of the registry or Windows directory.

Until the release of Windows Vista and Windows Server 2008, the Power Users group was often used as an alternative to the full administrator group in an attempt to restrict the privileges being granted. This group featured some privileges designed to give users specific administrator rights and permissions to perform everyday system tasks.

In subsequent operating system releases, Microsoft altered the default configuration, so that members of this group have no more user rights or permissions than those of a standard user account. This was primarily made possible because in later Windows versions, standard user accounts now feature the ability to perform most common configuration tasks, such as changing time zones, by default.

However additional custom groups may be defined and specific privileges, referred to as user rights assignments, may be granted through configuration (often using Group Policy, discussed later), either to individuals and both custom or existing built-in groups.

### What are the considerations for using this feature?

Where a specific privilege is required, these capabilities permit these to be assigned to a user, allowing them to perform a given task. The most significant challenge is that these privileges are granted broadly to the user themselves, thereby allowing any application they execute to use them and potentially exposing the system to significant risks. A simple example may be the SE_Backup privilege described previously, but many others may exist depending upon the rights being granted.

Similarly, it is challenging to identify which privileges are required to support a specific operation or application, as tools to support this type of discovery are not provided natively in Windows and it typically requires a significant effort to troubleshoot.

*What are the limitations of this feature?*

These configurations can prove challenging to deploy and manage (as well as configure) and must be targeted to devices, which then target the user or group that receives those privileges on the target system.

Whilst Group Policy natively supports configuring user rights assignments, creating tailored settings for discrete user roles – particularly for large volumes of roles – becomes hugely complicated and cumbersome not only to define and manage but also to support. It is also common that a privilege alone is not enough to allow an application to run or a task to be performed, complicating the process further.

Similarly, for those organisations operating under a modern IT management approach (described in more detail later), these configuration settings must be defined using a Configuration Service Provider (CSP) based configuration and delivered using an MDM technology, such as Microsoft's own InTune. Whilst System Centre Configuration Manager may be used to deliver CSPs, it requires an additional WMI-to-CSP bridge to support it.

## MICROSOFT PRIVILEGE MANAGEMENT – PERMISSIONS (ACCESS CONTROLS)

*What is this feature?*

In the Windows environment, permissions are the means of authorising users and groups to access objects, both locally on an endpoint and also across a network. Permissions are a broad and complex topic beyond the scope of this book, but are comprised of several concepts, including:

- The principle of Least Privilege; as it relates to the different levels of access which may be required to an object (e.g. read-only, modify, etc.).

- Permissions Inheritance; which allows permissions to flow down from a parent object into its child objects to simplify administration and maintain security

- Object Ownership; as creators of an object are afforded different privileges over it, even when permissions inheritance may generally grant specific permissions

- Object management and auditing;

- Combined Permissions; where multiple permissions sets may apply to control access to an object, for example, those applied to a folder and to the share of that folder

These permissions are defined by an access control entry (ACE) which describes a user (or trustee) and the access rights allowed, denied, or audited for them when they attempt to access an object. Multiple ACEs can be defined and are stored within a discretionary access control list (ACL) which itself is stored in the security descriptor for a securable object. I did say it was a complex topic!

These permissions are one of the primary techniques employed by Windows to prevent standard users from modifying or tampering with settings or folders within the environment. As such, they form a critical part of the security of a Windows environment.

### *What does this feature deliver?*

These access controls offer an extraordinarily granular and highly flexible set of configuration options, allowing you to selectively grant access to objects, even to un-privileged standard users. This can be used to grant unprivileged users the ability modify configuration files, for example, which are stored in protected locations where they do not ordinarily have access.

Given the pervasive use of these controls in enforcing restrictive controls throughout the environment, they may also be used to grant access to many facets of the Windows environment.

While file and folder permissions are perhaps the most obvious application of this approach, and will form part of supporting users performing privileged tasks from a standard user account, this also extends into the system registry. Even access to Windows Services is controlled through discretionary access control lists (DACLs), which may be modified to allow users to stop, start, restart and configure individual services.

### *What are the considerations for using this feature?*

Whilst permissions are a robust security mechanism that is heavily scrutinised for weaknesses due to its use, it is possible to fundamentally undermine the system security and other security tools which are built upon it by modifying permissions. Therefore, any modifications must be made with caution and after careful consideration of their implications.

Identifying what changes are required is another significant consideration. Microsoft provides a wide range of tools to assist you in defining what controls are enforced,both locally and through group policy. However, you must know in advance what settings you wish to configure. Many legacy applications write configuration files into protected OS locations (e.g. C:\Windows), but it is both time consuming and complex to triage each of these applications and implement all of the necessary configurations.

It is also worth remembering that when granting permissions (either to an individual or a group of users), those permissions always apply to them and any application running like them. This means they are not aware of the context in which the permissions are being used and any application executed as the user (including malware) will have the same level of access.

*What are the limitations of this feature?*

These restrictions are enforced by the Windows filesystem. However, as noted earlier, these permissions can often be overridden by a variety of privileges. As an example, the SE_TAKEOWNERSHIP privilege allows a user to become the owner of a file and re-write all of its permissions – potentially granting themselves access and locking out others.

Many of these privileges (including SE_TAKEOWNERSHIP and SE_BACKUP) are granted to members of the endpoint's local Administrators group by default, highlighting a fundamental challenge when attempting to restrict the actions of privileged users.

Similarly, these restrictions are only enforced when Windows is running. If users can access the filesystem outside of Windows, for example using bootable media, they can modify any part of it without any restriction. This can be addressed by implementing a complementary control such as drive encryption, including Window's BitLocker.

## MICROSOFT PRIVILEGE MANAGEMENT – USER ACCOUNT CONTROL (UAC)

*What is this feature?*

Whilst historically many have been critical of Microsoft's approach to security, Microsoft introduced User Account Control (UAC) with Vista/ Windows Server 2008 in response to the risks identified for operating under a local administrator account.

UAC is not a single component, but instead is a collection of technologies working together. Its objective is to enable users and system admins to run with standard user privileges most of the time but to use elevated rights simply and easily when required.

UAC attempts to detect when a process requires administrative rights and to elevate it once consent has been given by the end user (if "Admin Approval Mode" is configured). This considerably reduces the risks involved in running with an administrative account, when compared with the alternative of running with full-time admin rights, but it does not remove the threat entirely.

Additionally, UAC provides a more user-friendly means for standard users to be prompted when they need assistance in performing a privileged task, although obviously, they will always require another user with administrative privileges on their endpoint (e.g. a helpdesk engineer) to complete their elevated activity.

### What does this feature deliver?

To fully understand the benefits and drawbacks of UAC, it is important to discuss the key concepts on which it is built. The descriptions provided below assume UAC is enabled on an endpoint.

## Access tokens

An access token is generated by the Windows logon process after the user has successfully authenticated to the endpoint (locally or remotely) and contains information about the identity and privileges associated with a user account.

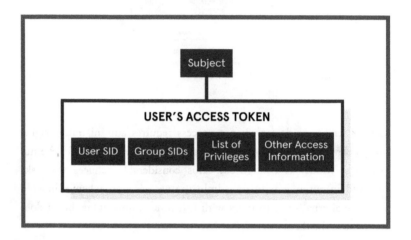

The logon process returns the security identifier (SID) for the user along with a list of SIDs for the security groups of which the user is a member.

The Local Security Authority (LSA) on the endpoint then uses this data to create an access token, known as the "primary access token".

The initial token is built using the user's SID, the SIDs of all of the groups of which the user is a member, and also the list of privileges assigned to the user or to the security groups they are a member of.

A copy of this primary access token is attached to (and inherited by) every process and thread that executes on the user's behalf. Whenever those applications (threads or processes) interact with a securable object (see permissions section earlier), or tries to perform a task that requires privileges (see privileges section earlier), the operating system checks the assigned access token to establish whether the action should be permitted. If permission is granted, it defines, what operations (read, write/modify, etc.) the requesting application is allowed to perform.

## Standard user Access Token

When a standard user logs into Windows (Vista and above), Windows Explorer is launched with the standard user's access token. However, when the user needs to elevate an application, they will be prompted to enter alternative credentials to start the process with a user account that has the required administrative rights.

In this scenario, the elevated process is running with a different access token than that of the standard user who logged in and started the desktop session, much the same as in earlier versions of Windows when the 'Run as administrator' option is used.

However, not only does an elevated process run with a different security access token, but it will also run in the context (under the identity) of another user account. Therefore, it may not have the same level of access to the local and remote resources as the standard user.

This illustrates one of several issues of using secondary administrative accounts to support the privilege use requirements of a standard user.

## Protected administrator accounts (Filtered Tokens)

UAC implements a Protected Administrator (PA) account to reduce the risks associated with logging on as an administrator. This functionality is implemented when UAC's "admin approval" mode is enabled.

This process works by issuing a "filtered" security access token that only grants standard user privileges until an application requires higher privileges, where the application can instead be run with a token containing full administrative rights.

Essentially the user is granted two tokens – one with administrative rights and one without.

When a Protected Administrator logs on, Explorer is launched with the filtered version of the user's access token. This filtered access token removes all administrative rights and renders it effectively the same as an access token issued to a standard user.

Any processes the user launches are also run with the filtered token unless a request for elevation is made and the user gives consent.

UAC's admin approval mode consent can be requested from the user in a variety of ways[22]:

22    https://docs.microsoft.com/en-us/windows/security/identity-protection/user-account-control/user-account-control-security-policy-settings

## Elevate without prompting

- Allows privileged accounts to perform an operation that requires elevation without requiring consent or credentials.

## Prompt for credentials on the secure desktop

- When an operation requires elevation of privilege, the user is prompted on the secure desktop to enter a privileged username and password. If the user enters valid credentials, the operation continues with the user's highest available privilege.

## Prompt for consent on the secure desktop

- When an operation requires elevation of privilege, the user is prompted on the secure desktop to select either Permit or Deny. If the user selects Permit, the operation continues with the user's highest available privilege.

## Prompt for credentials

- When an operation requires elevation of privilege, the user is prompted to enter an administrative username and password. If the user enters valid credentials, the operation continues with the applicable privilege.

## Prompt for consent

- When an operation requires elevation of privilege, the user is prompted to select either Permit or Deny. If the user selects Permit, the operation continues with the user's highest available privilege.

## Prompt for consent for non-Windows binaries (Default)

• When an operation for a non-Microsoft application requires elevation of privilege, the user is prompted on the secure desktop to select either Permit or Deny. If the user selects Permit, the operation continues with the user's highest available privilege.

Admin Approval Mode runs elevated processes with the same user account and security access token as the user who started the desktop session. The default configuration is to provide consent for elevation by clicking continue.

Alternatively, protected administrators can be forced to re-enter their credentials. This can be useful to force users to stop and think for a moment about what they are doing, rather than blindly clicking on a consent elevation prompt.

Running an application in the same security context mitigates the issues highlighted previously with the "Run as" approach.

## Windows Integrity Levels

Windows Integrity Levels and User Interface Privilege Isolation were introduced as part of UAC to help prevent malicious processes (those that run using the standard user/filtered access token of a Protected Administrator) injecting code into other processes that have been elevated to run with the unfiltered administrative token of the same Protected Administrator account.

The standard Windows security model prevents this type of attack when processes are being run using different user accounts, but as Protected Administrators operate with a split token, when they give a process consent to run with full administrative rights, it does so using the same user account.

Windows Integrity Levels assign a level of trust to all objects and processes, preventing those with a low level of trust from accessing objects and processes with a higher level of trust (integrity). Even if you decide to disable UAC, it still works. Processes running with lower integrity cannot perform the following actions on processes running with higher integrity:

1. Inject dynamic link libraries (DLLs)
2. Perform Windows handle validation
3. Monitor a process with journal hooks
4. Use SendMessage or PostMessage functions
5. Attach to a process using thread hooks

## Elevation prompts

As discussed, User Account Control attempts to simplify the process of elevating privileges by providing two different types of elevation prompts, depending on whether the user is running as a standard user or a Protected Administrator.

Auto-elevation means users do not usually have to decide which processes should run with administrative rights. Also, it removes the need to right-click on an executable and select 'Run as administrator' to elevate a program.

## Consent prompts

With the default configuration of Vista and Windows 7, when a user is running with a protected administrator account in Admin Approval Mode, if a process is elevated, a consent prompt is presented. The user is required to either grant or deny permission for the process to run with administrative rights by clicking Continue or Cancel.

## Credential prompts

When running as a standard user, you are required to enter the credentials of an administrative account to launch a process with elevated privileges (often referred to as Over the Shoulder or OTS prompts). Prompts may be colour-coded to give the user visual clues as to whether the application is potentially a risk, such as if it has not been digitally signed.

Both the Consent Prompts and Credentials Prompts are displayed on a "Secure Desktop" (by default). This helps protect the elevation prompt from being attacked by malware, as only Windows processes can access the secure desktop, thus helping to protect the privilege credentials.

## Filesystem and registry virtualisation

UAC's Filesystem and registry virtualisation help legacy applications run as a standard user by automatically redirecting attempts to perform read and write operations against protected areas of the filesystem and registry (e.g. %ProgramFiles%, %ProgramData%, and %SystemRoot%). These are redirected to a per-user virtual store which the user has permission to modify. However, this feature does not apply to 64-bit apps, services and Kernel-mode processes, such as drivers.

**Pros:**

- Merges the physical with the virtualised location to present a consist view
- Deleting virtualised files from within applications is supported
- Offers basic file and registry redirection

**Cons**

- Does not support multiple users who log onto the system, as application files are redirected to the user's profile and thus cannot be accessed by other users

- Virtualisation only works for a handful of folders and registry keys. It does not cover other 'admin' APIs, which if called from the non-admin app will cause the app to crash. The only way to solve this is to give the user administrative rights or modify the app not to make those calls

- Does not virtualise executables, i.e. if they are copied to the location

## Securing Internet Explorer (IE)

Protected Mode in Internet Explorer (the default mode) helps to defend against malware by utilising Windows Integrity Level. IE runs with low integrity, meaning it cannot write or read processes running with a higher-level of integrity. By default, all standard user processes run with medium integrity and all administrator processes run with high. Therefore, malware that may launch from an infected website would not be able to interact with processes outside of IE.

### What are the considerations for using this feature?

If users make extensive use of administrative privileges throughout their working day, when UAC is configured in the most secure manner (which causes the user to be prompted for authorisation for every privilege use), it can negatively impact the user's experience and become frustrating. The result of this impact (as seen in response to the default UAC settings in Vista) is that controls are relaxed to a less secure stance in order to deliver an acceptable user experience.

The configuration of UAC can be managed centrally through tools such as Group Policy; however, when they are not enforced through these mechanisms, users who operate with local administrative privileges can change these settings to minimise the prompts or disable UAC entirely. This means that all their processes will run with full administrative privileges.

Similarly, even when users are prompted continuously, the effectiveness of the prompts is reduced as users become so used to their appearance during "normal" tasks, they will frequently click through them without reviewing the associated details. This can obviously allow unintended elevation of applications, including malware.

As UAC makes some significant changes to the Windows security environment, it can have compatibility implications for certain applications, most commonly legacy applications. This can ultimately prevent UAC from being enabled at all on some endpoints. Additionally, legacy applications that require shared data access among some users may fail due to the file and registry virtualisation features.

There are also many applications, including parts of the Windows OS (e.g. Device Manager) which are not "UAC aware". This prevents UAC from being able to identify when they require elevated rights and often requires users to take manual steps to force an application to run elevated, for example by using the "Run as administrator" option provided via the Windows right-click context menu.

### *What are the limitations of this feature?*

One of the most significant limitations of the UAC implementation is that there is no granular control over which applications can and cannot be elevated - it is essentially "all-or-nothing". From an enterprise perspective, this is compounded by the limited visibility of when, where and why users choose to elevate activities. Even when correctly configured, UAC auditing is tied to the use of UAC's consent dialog, meaning that depending upon how UAC is configured, you may not see all of the user's activity.

From Windows 7 onwards, Microsoft configured UAC's default behaviour to auto-elevate Windows binaries which request elevated rights. This minimises the number of prompts a user must interact with to only third party applications which request elevated rights.

However, this means that some built-in Windows programs always run privileged, which can provide a means for attackers to bypass UAC's protections to execute malicious code with elevated rights, without any consent being required from a user.

These bypass techniques only work in this way when UAC is not configured to always prompt the user. Unfortunately, as noted above, this option is rarely used due to the overly intrusive impact upon the user's experience. Additionally, Microsoft states that UAC is not a security boundary and as such, it does not consider the ability to bypass it a critical flaw and will not implement a fix.

| Feature | UAC |
| --- | --- |
| Control Mechanism | User driven, there is no central control of what can and can't be elevated |
| Administrative Account Required | Yes (or access to one) |
| Privileges Assigned | Full administrative rights |
| Privilege Inheritance | Child processes always inherits the elevated rights of the parent |
| On Demand | Always available (run as) |
| Application Types | Executables, installers |
| Auditing | Very limited |
| Application Forensics | No |
| Custom Messaging | No (fixed messages) |
| User Request | No ability to integrate with central work flows. |
| Platforms | Windows Vista and above |

# MICROSOFT PRIVILEGE MANAGEMENT
# – APPLICATION COMPATIBILITY TOOLKIT
# (APPLICATION SHIMS)

### *What is this feature?*

To allow new Microsoft Operating Systems to be developed, while still retaining compatibility with legacy applications often used by enterprises, Microsoft designed the Windows Application Compatibility Infrastructure.

This toolset was initially released with Windows XP to help system administrators solve compatibility problems for applications that were designed to run in earlier versions of Windows. Often these compatibility problems were the product of poor coding practices and product design, but were compounded by security improvements designed to protect the endpoint.

Often these poor design and coding practices require the user to run them with full administrative privileges.

### *What does this feature deliver?*

The toolkit allows you to create compatibility fixes, known as "shims", to target specific problems within the legacy application, allowing them to run under modern OS versions.

The advantage of implementing shims is that rather than maintaining the legacy code within the operating system, the legacy application code is instead modified via the shim. This makes the OS inherently less complicated, more secure and easier to support.

When a shim is applied to an application, it intercepts the Win32 API calls from legacy applications and modifies it before passing the code onwards to Windows to execute, ensuring they are compatible with the APIs available within the modern OS.

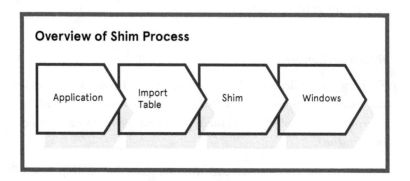

**Overview of Shim Process**

Application → Import Table → Shim → Windows

## Out of the box compatibility shims

Windows itself natively includes a default set of compatibility modes. These can be used without the need to create custom shims, but as you would expect, they are limited in their capabilities.

Windows Vista and above include the Program Compatibility Assistant, which attempts to automate the process of applying compatibility fixes to legacy applications by monitoring for known problems and prompting the user to apply a recommended fix.

**These fixes can address:**

- Errors when launching setup programs
- Failures in install routines
- Failures caused by UAC
- Installs needing to run as an administrator
- Control panel applets requiring administrative rights
- Errors caused because a component is not present in the current version of Windows

**Additionally, the tool can be used to:**

- Match applications against a list of programs with known problems and notify the user at program start-up
- Notify users about unsigned drivers on 64-bit versions of Windows

One of the most common use-cases for shims is to address the need to run legacy applications as an administrator. However, this is typically not a straightforward problem to resolve.

As discussed in earlier sections, system administrators may choose to grant users administrative rights to users or loosen Access Control Lists (ACLs) on files, directories, or registry keys to ensure legacy applications will run. These approaches undoubtedly increase the attack surface of an endpoint and make it more likely to be compromised by malicious threats, both internal and external.

Shims, on the other hand, do not require users to hold any additional privileges and do not need any modification of the systems security settings. Consequently, shims offer a far more secure alternative to the workarounds described previously.

### What are the considerations for using this feature?

One of the features of a shim is the ability to redirect access requests to protected areas of the filesystem and registry to a virtualised location. However, this approach can introduce a new set of problems, especially on shared machines, due to the issues discussed with UAC virtualisation previously.

On security principles, I would always recommend a shim over weakening ACLs in an attempt to solve compatibility problems, as this is infinitely more secure. Read and write operations are the most common reason why legacy programs fail, but there are many others and shims provide a solution for a whole host of compatibility issues that weakening ACLs cannot solve.

Windows interprets the modified code presented to it by the shim as code from the application itself. Therefore, application code modified by a shim runs in the same security context as the application and cannot be used to bypass Windows security features.

*What are the limitations of this feature?*

As alluded to above, there are some implications to the use of shims that often prevent them from being successfully adopted, particularly in enterprise environments. The following describes some of the challenges and highlights why the less desirable workaround approaches discussed previously are often chosen instead.

## Developer level application knowledge

The Application Compatibility toolkit requires a developer or system administrator who is familiar with development studios and the application's behaviour to build shims. Once built, an extensive amount of testing must take place to ensure the application works as expected. For all but the largest organisations, this functionality remains elusive; many system administrators are not aware of their existence or do not know how to use shims.

 I have seen instances of shims being deployed to live environments only to find they break weeks or months down the line, usually because the application has not been fully tested and the end users have triggered the issue by using obscure application features.

## Deployment headaches

The shims themselves need to be distributed, either with the application's installer or to the machines affected by the issue. In small environments where only a few legacy applications require shims, it may be feasible to package a custom database with each application. If many applications require shims, a more scalable solution is to maintain a single central custom database and update it on the client machines.

These can be deployed using a Group Policy start-up script. In large organisations, I have seen several sets of custom databases deployed to defined categories of users for ease of administration. In addition, you could consider adding a custom database to the OS image. For all of these reasons, shims can be challenging to create, manage and deploy.

## Kernel-mode applications

Shims cannot be used to solve compatibility problems with drivers and other software that hooks deep into the operating system. Shims run in user-mode, so the vendor must modify drivers and kernel-mode software if there are compatibility problems.

## Vendor support

Essentially, shims mean you are modifying an application's behaviour and therefore run the risk of invalidating any support agreement with the vendor. You should check in advance whether support would be provided if a shim were used to solve a compatibility problem. Of course, in an ideal world, the vendor should fix the problem. However, it is not uncommon for vendors to refuse to investigate an issue until the applied shim has been removed.

I have been in situations in the past where vendors have directly refused to look at an issue until the applied shim has been removed, even though it was unlikely to be the cause of the problem.

## MODIFYING THE FILE SYSTEM TO FORCE APPLICATIONS TO RUN

In some cases (but not all) privilege problems related to files, folders, and registry keys can be solved by weakening permissions using Windows Sysinternals tools, such as Process Monitor and Group Policy.

### Process Monitor

If applications need to write to protected registry keys or files but do not have the necessary permissions, you can use Process Monitor from Technet's Sysinternals website to identify the problem files or registry keys. This application will display the files, folders and registry keys an application is trying to access or write to. From here, you will be able to establish any "access denied" issues the application is facing.

### Apply the workarounds with Group Policy

The following Group Policy setting - Computer Configuration -> Windows Settings > Security Settings - can be configured to apply changes to multiple computers. I would recommend creating a new Group Policy Object (GPO) to test the settings and apply this to an Organisational Unit (OU) containing a group of test machines prior to any production-wide rollout.

Please note that any changes you make to permissions on files, folders and registry keys will also be available to other applications running in the context of the logged on users. I have seen malware infect machines because of the above procedure. Essentially, you are opening up security holes in your OS to force an application to work, so caution is always advised.

## LEAST VS. LESS PRIVILEGE

### Temporary administrative accounts

Windows does not have any built-in mechanism that allows the temporary granting of administrative rights, leaving organisations apprehensive about committing to least privilege. In this section, we will look at a couple of common techniques that I have seen used to grant temporary administrative access.

A primary concern for most organisations is how to support users in break glass situations that require administrator privileges. There are hundreds of examples of these scenarios, from remote workers being at conferences, to research staff needing to test new software.

## Secondary administrative accounts – Good in principle, bad in practice

I often come across organisations that give users two accounts - one with administrative access and one without. The logic behind this is that users will log on with the standard user account and use the 'Run As' administrative function to elevate applications and functions as and when needed. However, in reality, the user generally stays logged in with their administrative account or uses this account to add themselves back to the local admins group.

Luckily, many things can be done to prevent this, such as prohibiting the administrative account from accessing email servers and the internet. This often involves firewall and e-mail server tweaks. You can also configure Group Policy to reset the local user and groups database via the "Restricted Groups GPO or Group Policy preferences". However, with access to a local administrative account, it is possible to disable Group Policy within 30 seconds!

 Secondary logon service: Windows 2000 introduced the Secondary Logon Service and Run As command, which were intended for system administrators in the hope that they would log on as a standard user and elevate privileges only when required for administrative tasks.

# MICROSOFT PRIVILEGE MANAGEMENT – JUST ENOUGH ADMIN (JEA)

*What is this feature?*

Whilst many of the features discussed so far in this chapter span both desktop and server environments, the Just Enough Admin (JEA) capability is squarely focussed on the Windows Server environment.

Specifically, it is designed to remove the need for users to log in with administrative privileges, to limit the scope of what users can do and to audit their actions to provide accountability. JEA achieves this by allowing server users to perform designated administrative tasks on the specified server, using PowerShell, without needing to give those users full local administrator rights.

This may be used to address these challenges for a wide variety of users, both internal such as helpdesk users and server administrators, as well as external and third party engineers who may also need to perform specific privileged operations within an enterprises server environment.

JEA is based on a Windows PowerShell feature called "constrained run spaces", a technology which is used extensively within Microsoft's own environments (including Office 365) to help control and limit administrative tasks being performed.

*What does this feature deliver?*

JEA provides a role-based approach to define capabilities and controls for technical IT users, providing a standardised method of reducing administrative access and their associated risks, with more granularity and visibility than traditional access control models.

JEA uses the built-in capabilities of the Windows PowerShell scripting environment, allowing any task or command which could be performed through PowerShell, including those to be managed and performed through JEA securely.

Role capabilities are used to define the PowerShell cmdlets, functions scripts and providers that a user may need to perform. A session configuration is used to define which users may use a JEA endpoint and which role capabilities they can use, as well as defining settings such as auditing transcripts.

The final step is to register the JEA endpoint using the role capabilities and session configuration described above. This process applies the session configuration information to the system and makes the endpoint available for use by users and automation engines.

This process enables authorised users to run specific commands in an elevated context on a remote machine, complete with full PowerShell transcription and logging. This may be performed using the native PowerShell remoting capabilities or through the PowerShell web interface.

### *What are the considerations for using this feature?*

JEA is available across a large number of Windows client and server operating systems, but requires that the Windows Management Framework v5.0 is installed and that the version of PowerShell installed is at least version 5.0.

Each JEA endpoint has a designated "run as" account, which is the account under which the connecting user's actions are performed. This account is configurable in the session configuration file, and the account you choose has a significant bearing on the security of your endpoint.

Perhaps the most significant challenge with JEA is actually defining the role capabilities, as it requires an intimate knowledge of the specific commands that the users need to perform. It is extremely common for enterprises to have little visibility of the applications system administrators use, let alone the specific commands.

Finally, in order to adopt this approach, the system administrators must be familiar with the fundamental operation of PowerShell, as well as the specific syntax and parameters of commands.

### What are the limitations of this feature?

One of the most significant limitations of JEA is that it is limited to PowerShell and the use of a command line interface. A challenge which was even faced by Microsoft while implementing JEA was that many system administrators are still accustomed to using GUIs rather than the Windows PowerShell command-line shell and scripting environment. Similarly, there are many third party remote management tools which cannot be utilised through JEA.

## PRIVILEGED IDENTITY MANAGEMENT (PIM) – THE ROLE OF VAULTING AND SESSION RECORDING

Many businesses, financial institutions and regulated authorities have implemented a Privileged Identity Management (PIM) or Identity and Access Management (IAM) solution to address regulatory requirements for the monitoring of privileged user activity. These solutions are especially relevant and powerful for servers which are controlled by IT/system administrators (sysadmins).

Such solutions are traditionally designed to grant secure access to specific destinations through a password vault. When a sysadmin requests access to a specific server, the vault will grant it by providing a temporary administrative account and then begin recording the session. Access rights will be given for the duration of the session until the task is completed and the session is closed.

Such systems were later expanded to control application run time privileges, thus obscuring run time credentials from the user and the application. However, this requires the application vendor to make use of API calls into the vault to check out the appropriate credentials when needed.

The key benefits of such solutions come from the tight control of login credentials, ensuring the sysadmin/application never has visibility of the password. This increases the organisation's security defences against unauthorised configuration changes, data compromise and other insider threats.

Additionally, session recording is used to ensure that regulated companies have the tools to meet their audit requirements for the monitoring of privileged activity.

However, session recording alone is inadequate when adhering to many audit requirements, security policies, or indeed, the more advanced internal and external threats that are facing organisations every day.

These solutions, when used in isolation, simply do not provide enough protection. Assuming that sysadmins do not attempt to hide their unauthorised activity, any damage captured in recording has already been done. The challenge for IT teams is to find a solution that enhances and complements their existing vaulting and session recording technology.

To be most effective in terms of security, productivity and resource, these solutions must be combined with granular endpoint privilege elevation and delegation technologies, ensuring sysadmins and applications are controlled. By combining vaulting and endpoint technologies, organisations can increase their security defences and take a more proactive stance to combat today's advanced threats.

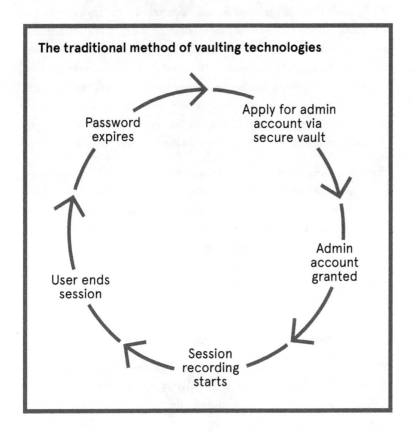

**The traditional method of vaulting technologies**

- Apply for admin account via secure vault
- Admin account granted
- Session recording starts
- User ends session
- Password expires

  "60% all attacks in 2015 were carried out by insiders. 44.5% malicious, 15.5% inadvertent actors."

— IBM Cyber Security Intelligence Index [23]

23  http://www-01.ibm.com/common/ssi/cgi-bin/ssialias?subtype=WH&infotype=SA&htmlfid=
SEW03133USEN&attachment=SEW03133USEN.PDF

*What are the considerations of PIM?*

## Administrator accounts are issued

When vault controls are used in isolation, an administrator account is still issued for the duration of the session. The dangers of administrator privileges have been well-documented in this book and many other papers, acting as the back door into the heart of the business and its data. Administrator accounts are frequently targeted by hackers and malware, with the potential to be exploited by insiders (whether through deliberate or unintentional misuse). Sysadmins are the most powerful form of user, with full and unrestricted access to perform any task.

However, when credential vaults are coupled with endpoint privilege elevation and delegation technologies, domain-wide and local permissions can be abstracted from the user and fine-grain local admin privileges can be granted on a per-user, per-server basis. Therefore, sysadmins can log onto the server sessions with a standard user account, and privileges can be granted for specific applications, tasks and scripts. If enterprise-wide credentials are needed, the vault can be contacted, and the applications can be executed under these credentials.

## Administrator sessions can be left active

Typically, vaults and recording use logon and logoff triggers to identify the beginning and end of a session. It is possible for sysadmins to circumnavigate or bypass the controls by simply 'disconnecting' their session, leaving it running so they can reconnect later. Therefore it is important that the vaulting technology in use can proactively kill any orphaned sessions.

## Session recording is a reactive security measure

Session recording captures the steps taken during the open session in CCTV-style fashion so that if a breach was to occur, the footage could be examined to establish the cause. The flaw in session recording as a standalone solution can be summarised in the analogy of a bank robbery: CCTV records the crime, and the perpetrator might later be identified and apprehended from the documented evidence. But while acting as a deterrent, the recording does not prevent the crime from happening in the first place. The same applies when dealing with data, but unlike a bank robbery, perpetrators can infiltrate a network days, weeks or months before any damage is done.

The challenge for many organisations is in the storage and management of session recordings, which represent a substantial resource impact - both regarding physical storage and for employees to review and manually annotate hours of footage.

**Ask yourself the following questions to help establish if session recording is really the answer:**

- Who is looking at these recordings?
- Does the reviewer understand what they are looking at?
- What is INSIDE that script named "UpdateSettings.ps1" that was run? Did they add a local admin account in the script or schedule some additional tasks to run later on?
- Check whether the solution can annotate the recordings: when combined with endpoint privilege elevation and delegation technologies, it may be possible to annotate the recording at specific points where privileges were used.
- Has the horse bolted? Were organisational interests compromised? If it has, then damage control starts now.

## Regulations are becoming more stringent

In the past, heavily regulated industries would implement PIM solutions to meet compliance mandates which stipulated least privilege. In recent years I have seen many regulatory bodies tighten up their controls and no longer accept PIM solutions as a complete answer. They are now mandating that endpoint privilege elevation and delegation controls must also be in place.

## Application runtime privileges

In many cases, vaults will provide a set of APIs to allow application vendors to check out credentials at runtime. This allows applications to leverage privileges without the user or the applications having access to the credentials i.e. when an application needs to query a database. This is a great solution, as long as the application vendor has written the application to work in this way. In many cases the vendor has not. Therefore, look for endpoint elevation and delegation solutions that integrate with vaults, can check out application runtime credentials, and execute the application under these credentials. This is a great way to control what can execute, and under which credentials. It also means that no credentials have to be stored in config files and thus cannot be stolen.

### Summary

PIM solutions (vaulting/session monitoring solutions) have an important place in your security strategy, but they should be deployed in conjunction with endpoint controls, removing the need to grant local administrator accounts. As we have already discussed, removing excess administrative rights is one of the most essential risk mitigation strategies. Once administrator account use can be controlled, consideration can be given to PIM type solutions, as there will be specific accounts which need to be vaulted, such as Enterprise Admin and application run time accounts.

Dealing with the overuse of administrator accounts also expedites the implementation of PIM solutions, as there will be fewer accounts to on-board - thus speeding up your deployments.

# VIRTUAL DESKTOP INFRASTRUCTURE – HOW CAN THIS HELP LEAST PRIVILEGE?

While it is always best to avoid virtualisation technologies to solve compatibility fixes, in the real world that is not always possible. Virtual Desktop Infrastructure (VDI) provides organisations that do not have the technical resources or time to solve compatibility issues with a fast, if not ideal, solution.

There are many VDI technologies in this space and to discuss them all is outside the scope of this book. Typically, you will see VDI deployed and managed via technologies from VMware, such as ESX technology, and Hyper-V from Microsoft. All of these technologies provide a way to virtualise and deliver an OS to the user over the network.

The critical thing to remember is that these are full OS' and in most cases will be joined or have access to your network. Therefore, you are shifting the problem from the user's local machine into the data centre.

Clients often tell me that all their users are standard users and they have Application Control applied to their machines, only to find each of their developers has a VDI machine on which they are an admin and can do whatever they like. These machines need to be managed in the same way that any other device would be.

## Virtualising Applications

Application Virtualisation is a technology that allows applications to be run on virtualised layers that are isolated from each other and the operating system. This can help to alleviate compatibility issues and problems related to privileges. Microsoft offers a technology called Application Virtualisation (App-V). Other vendors provide similar technology but broadly speaking the concepts, advantages and disadvantages are the same.

Applications run in dedicated virtualisation layers, and there's no need to deploy virtual machines, which saves a lot of time. Applications are streamed from an on-premises server or across the internet, as well as being available offline. They can also be managed centrally so that if an application is updated on the server, those changes are automatically streamed to clients.

These tools work by creating a virtualised bubble for each application. Each bubble isolates an application from the host operating system and from other applications. System services (Windows services, COM, OLE, printers, fonts, cut and paste), files (DLLs, .ini files, and so on), and registry keys are all virtualised in separate bubbles. The virtualised programs' calls are redirected to virtualised resources i.e. system services, files, and registry keys. This enables programs to run without actually being installed on the host operating system.

**Using this technology on the desktop we can:**

- Eliminate conflicts with other applications running on the same host OS

- Allow legacy applications that require administrative rights to run with a standard user account

- Run different versions of the same application on the same host OS

- Update applications on a central server and stream the changes to desktops

- Allow standard users to run applications on demand without the need to elevate to administrative rights

- Only stream the required elements of an application suite

- Enable applications to follow users who work on multiple devices

## Using App-V to help with administrative rights

Standard users are able to modify the application's virtual registry or filesystem within a virtual bubble, as there are no Access Control Lists (ACLs) that prevent this. This means that most programs will have no privilege issues within a virtual bubble. If a virtual program is allowed to pass through to the host OS to read or write to a file or registry key, ACLs apply to the logged-in user as if the application was running locally on the host OS, and therefore could still have issues.

Virtual packages can provide a way of enabling user self-service, where users can choose which applications to install and when to install them. This can all be done without administrative rights.

### *What are the limitations of this approach?*

Application Virtualisation gives organisations the ability to deploy secure, but at the same time, flexible systems. I have had some great success with this, but in truth, it is not a panacea. Firstly, you need a licence for this technology. Secondly, you need to create, test and manage the virtual packages. This in itself is not the most natural thing to do, especially if the application requires access to the OS or needs to save data outside the virtual bubble. Although this can help in many ways, you will find that it is only viable where the time of creating packages is cost justifiable.

## 4.2. **Application whitelisting – typical tools and tech**
· · · · · · · · · · · · · · · · · · · · · · · · · · · · · · · · · · · · · · ·

In this section, I look at the tools that provide application whitelist capabilities.

## MICROSOFT – APPLICATION CONTROL

Microsoft Application Control functionality has evolved both iteratively with AppLocker and through more significant changes in the guise of Device Guard, yet still, only around ten per cent of Microsoft customers implement any Application Control capabilities.

These core capabilities have seen refinements to help with operationalisation and have been bolstered with additional technologies such as Windows Defender Application Control, Windows Defender Application Guard and Windows Defender Exploit Protection, all of which we will explore in more depth in the next sections.

It is perhaps also unsurprising that capabilities have been designed to work closely with Microsoft's other technologies, for example, centralised software distribution and management using technologies such as System Center Configuration Manager (SCCM).

# MICROSOFT APPLICATION CONTROL – APPLOCKER

*What is this feature?*

Replacing Software Restriction Policies (SRP) in Windows 7/Server 2008 R2, AppLocker was the primary application control capability offered natively within the Windows OS environment.

Whilst the number of Application Control tools and their capabilities have expanded with later OS versions, notably Windows 10, AppLocker remains an important tool when implementing user or role-specific application control restrictions within Windows. It is the only native Application Control functionality which can be targeted more granularly than the endpoint device as a whole.

*What does this feature deliver?*

AppLocker uses an Application Identity service to evaluate any process creation events, script executions or attempts to load a DLL. These actions are reviewed against a policy containing a number of rules which define what activities are permitted (whitelisted) and which are blocked (blacklisted). When implementing a default-deny whitelist, any application not explicitly whitelisted will be implicitly prevented from executing.

When restrictions are being enforced and a user is prevented from running a given application, Windows displays a notification message directing the user to their IT support staff for assistance.

**Rules can be applied to five different types, or collections, of files:**

- An executable rule controls whether a user or group can run an executable file, most commonly applications. Executable files most often have the .exe or .com file extension

- A script rule controls whether a user or group can run scripts, specifically files with any of the following extensions: .ps1, .bat, .cmd, .vbs, and .js.

- The Windows Installer rule controls whether a user or group can run files with a .msi, .mst and .msp extension.

- DLL rules control whether a user or group can run files with a file extension of .dll or .ocx.

- The packaged app and packaged app installer rule control whether a user or group can run or install a packaged app. These are most typically applications from the Windows store and feature the .appx extension.

**These files may be targeted using one of three different conditions, including:**

- A publisher condition on a rule controls whether a user or group can run files from a specific software publisher. These files must be signed directly in order to use this criterion.

- A path condition on a rule controls whether a user or group can run files from a specific directory, or one of its sub-directories.

- A file hash condition on a rule controls whether a user or group can run files with a matching Authenticode/SHA256 cryptographic hash.

- Some of these conditions allow additional attributes of the application to be evaluated, in order to match more specific instances of it, for example, a particular product or version of a piece of software signed by a specific application publisher.

These configurations must be distributed to the endpoints being secured, using native Active Directory Group Policy configuration settings, or through a Configuration Service Provider (CSP) based configuration. CSPs are delivered using an MDM technology such as Microsoft's own InTune. Whilst SCCM may be used to deliver CSPs, it requires an additional WMI-to-CSP bridge to support it.

### *What are the considerations for using this feature?*

A primary consideration is whether you can fully utilise AppLocker for your endpoints. Under earlier Windows versions (e.g. Windows 7/8) controls could only be enforced on Enterprise SKUs (versions), and whilst Windows 10 supports AppLocker across all SKUs, only the Enterprise and Education versions can be managed using Group Policy – all other SKUs can only be managed using an AppLocker CSP.

Next, we must consider the configuration, including its initial creation and ongoing management, as well as its distribution to end-user devices and how these factors relate to your ability to support changing end-user requirements.

As noted above, delivering policies to your endpoints may be challenging in itself. However, when we consider that a user's machine must be online (and potentially also connected to a VPN) to receive updated policy to run the new application they have downloaded, the challenge clearly emerges.

As staff increasingly work remotely, and cloud services reduce the need to connect back via VPNs, how can we hope to support user's changing requirements efficiently and effectively, whilst still maintaining good practice processes and procedures such as change control?

Microsoft's consultancy practice now embraces the pragmatic trust-based whitelisting model as a means to simplify initial configurations, which has been long advocated by many security experts, including the UK

National Cyber Security Centre (NCSC) in its end-user device (EUD) security guidance.

This approach uses directories within the OS, which restrict the user's write access by default (e.g. C:\Windows and C:\Program Files), as the foundation for building a whitelist. The logic of this method is that applications are typically installed or updated within these paths, so by approving anything in these locations, it negates the need to identify individual applications specifically.

Whilst this is a valid approach that negates many of the traditional headaches of a whitelisting, of which dealing with constantly changing applications is perhaps the greatest, it is fundamentally undermined if it is used on devices where users retain full administrative access, which allows them to modify the contents of those "trusted" paths.

Where this pragmatic approach cannot be taken, organisations must either use more explicit whitelisting (e.g. hash-based) with all its negative implications, or utilise AppLocker's "Managed Installer" feature to establish the trust of applications as they are deployed to the endpoint. This latter functionality is described in more detail later in this section.

Whilst publisher-based rules may appear to offer some hope to the above challenges, the vast majority of enterprises continue to use (and even develop themselves) software which does not include an Authenticode signature, forcing other techniques to be used instead. Perhaps the simplest solution to this particular challenge is for the organisation to include application signing as part of its software deployment processes, but this is an approach few (if any) take.

### *What are the limitations of this feature?*

The capabilities of AppLocker are designed to meet a specific set of requirements, and Microsoft acknowledges that AppLocker is not a security boundary. It was designed to help organisations with compliance challenges including which applications run within their environment.

Due to this status, Microsoft does not treat techniques which bypass AppLocker's restrictions as security vulnerabilities to be fixed, meaning that a wide range of such techniques exist and others continue to be developed which allow AppLocker's controls to be worked around.

These techniques also highlight some of the challenges organisations face by having to make trade-offs in what they permit their users to run and being limited by AppLocker's targeting capabilities. These prevent them approving specific usage, such as running an application with a specific command line or in a specific circumstance, whilst blocking abuse.

Most fundamentally, AppLocker's policies are open to manipulation if attackers are able to take up a privileged position within the endpoint environment, for example being able to execute code within the kernel mode. This specific challenge is one Device Guard - which I go into more detail about below - is designed to address.

If applications or operating system functions require administrative rights, organisations using AppLocker would still need to assign them to the user and thus open up systems to abuse. Essentially, it is not hard to bypass AppLocker. I have listed four ways to disable AppLocker below as an admin, none of which require you to be deeply tech-savvy:

1. Stop the Application Identity service (AppIDSvc)
2. Right-click an executable and choose "Run as Administrator."
3. Create Local AppLocker policies (which would then merge with the GPO settings)
4. Boot into SafeMode

**The table below details other areas of consideration.**

| Feature | AppLocker |
| --- | --- |
| Group Policy | Computer only |
| Application privileges | No – applications run in the context of the logged on user |
| Application control | Allow, deny |
| Application types | Executables, installers, scripts<br><br>Note: installers will rely on UAC if administrative rights required |
| Application rules | Path, hash, publisher |
| Auditing | Yes – basic |
| Application Forensics | No |
| Custom Messaging | No |
| User Request | No |
| Platforms | AppLocker is available in all editions of Windows Server 2008 R2 and in Windows 7 Ultimate and Windows 7 Enterprise. Windows 7 Professional can be used to create AppLocker rules. However, AppLocker rules cannot be enforced on computers running Windows 7 Professional.<br><br>Windows 8, Windows Server 2012 and Windows 10 |

## MICROSOFT APPLICATION CONTROL - DEVICE GUARD

When it was originally released as part of Windows 10, Device Guard was the name used to describe Code Integrity (CI) and Hypervisor Code Integrity (HVCI), a set of hardware and OS technologies which could be used together to lock down and tightly control an endpoint.

Since that point, "Device Guard" has undergone a re-branding, and rather than referring to these technologies, it now refers to the locked-down endpoint state that is achieved when implementing these features in their entirety.

This re-branding was largely to address customer confusion regarding the requirements of using these features. The HVCI capability, in particular, has hardware requirements which historically not all devices could meet. Where that was the case, many customers believed that this also meant they could not use the Code Integrity portion of Device Guard on those systems either.

The capabilities of the original "Device Guard" feature continue to exist, but they do so under new names which are intended to help customers better understand their capabilities and usage.

## MICROSOFT APPLICATION CONTROL – WINDOWS DEFENDER APPLICATION CONTROL

### *What is this feature?*

Prior to Microsoft re-launching this capability under the new branding of Windows Defender Application Control (WDAC), this was the

"Code Integrity" capability (aka Configurable Code Integrity) of Device Guard.

Code Integrity (CI) allows customers to set an application control policy that is enforced by the Windows Kernel itself, and which not only applies to code running in user mode, but also to kernel mode hardware and software drivers. It even extends to nearly all of the code that runs Windows itself.

These policies themselves can be signed to prevent even those with administrative accounts from tampering with them, and the CI feature is further complemented by the virtualisation-based security feature known as hypervisor protected code integrity (HVCI), as well as Platform and Unified Extensible Firmware Interface (UEFI) Secure Boot, both of which increase the security and protection derived from the Code Integrity policy.

This same technology is used within Windows 10 S to restrict what applications can execute on that platform.

### What does this feature deliver?

As the name suggests, CI is an Application Control capability at heart, but it fundamentally changes the trust model of the endpoint to require that all "code" (i.e. applications, scripts etc.) is signed and trusted, for it to be allowed to run. A default-deny state applies to any other code, and it simply cannot execute on the endpoint, in either kernel or user mode.

Whilst the approach of any unsigned or untrusted code being implicitly blocked is highly effective from a security perspective, particularly as historically most malware has been unsigned, it does provide some significant challenges in ensuring that legitimate code is signed. However, even if an application is not signed by its author, it can still be signed via a catalogue signature, which is a signed list of file hashes.

Creating a catalogue signature is achieved by first capturing the file hashes of the unsigned application in a catalogue file via the PackageInspector.exe tool. This catalogue can then be signed by uploading it to Microsoft's Device Guard signing portal, which isa single place to sign catalogue files and code integrity policies accessible via the Microsoft Store for Business and Microsoft Store for Education.

WDAC's core functionality and protection starts at the hardware level. Devices which have processors supporting virtualisation extensions and features, such as Second Layer Address Translation (SLAT), can take advantage of the Windows 10 Virtualization Based Security (VBS) environment to dramatically increase security through the isolation of critical Windows services from the operating system itself.

WDAC can leverage VBS to isolate its HVCI service, which helps protect kernel mode processes and drivers from vulnerability exploits and zero days. By using the processor's functionality, HVCI can force all software running in kernel mode to allocate memory and protect against code injection attacks safely.

### What are the considerations for using this feature?

Much like with AppLocker, Windows 10 supports WDAC across all SKUs (versions), but again, only the Enterprise and Education versions can be managed using Group Policy. All other SKUs can only be managed using an MDM platform such as Microsoft's InTune, using an endpoint protection profile.

The requirement for all code to be signed, either by the publisher via a signing catalogue, is not to be overlooked. Many organisations develop software internally which is often unsigned, in addition to the many legitimate (often legacy) applications which may exist throughout an environment which may also be unsigned by their authors.

This is not a task which will be completed only at the point of initial deployment, never to be repeated. Each time an application signed via a catalogue signature is updated, a new catalogue must be created to capture its new hash and allow it to execute. The process of creating and signing catalogues will, therefore, form part of the business as usual process of supporting the technology and will require a full workflow to ensure users aren't impacted (or to avoid the temptation not to patch).

It is also important to remember that these controls are defined and deployed system-wide, regardless of the user who is logging on. Therefore, if you wish to implement more granular user-based and role-specific controls, it is necessary to implement an AppLocker policy in conjunction with the WDAC configuration. It is also necessary to configure WDAC to the most permissive action required by any user who might log on to an endpoint, as an AppLocker allow rule will not override a WDAC deny.

### *What are the limitations of this feature?*

When attempting to deploy CI policies, the most significant issues often arise when looking to enforce (rather than simply audit) the restrictions they have defined. This often results in systems experiencing blue screens and rendering them unusable, and in some instances corrupt.

The complexities of this transition are almost always related to the unsigned code that exists within their environments, often including unsigned kernel drivers which ship with enterprise devices. These issues can be both challenging and time-consuming to troubleshoot, and given the diversity of enterprise devices, this can pose a potentially significant headache.

Similarly, the rate of change of software within an enterprise environment is significant with both internally developed and third party applications that must be managed through catalogue signing. Whilst features such as Managed Installer (discussed later in this chapter) may appear to help mitigate these challenges, due to some of its own limitations around updating application, these issues will often have to be resolved manually.

Finally, where AppLocker and WDAC are being used together to meet the requirements of an environment, it is worth noting that these two technologies are not integrated. As such, this process will require two discrete but interdependent configurations to be managed and maintained in parallel. This opens up the risk of a mismatched configuration state and the prospect of complex troubleshooting to identify the cause, in addition to doubling the management overhead. In many cases, WDAC also requires a reboot for any changes to take effect.

## MICROSOFT APPLICATION CONTROL – MANAGED INSTALLER

*What is this feature?*

One of the greatest challenges faced by organisations deploying both AppLocker and Device Guard application control policies is dealing with the ever-changing requirements of the user estate – the applications which appear on the whitelist. Both technologies are limited by their ability to handle dynamic changes - exceptions, in other words - meaning that new applications often require configuration changes to support them.

As more organisations have adopted software deployment technologies, such as Microsoft's System Center Configuration Manager (SCCM) to manage their software estate, Microsoft has developed a link between these distribution platforms and the Windows Application Control technologies. This link allows any applications deployed through these defined platforms to be automatically trusted by the application control technology.

### *What does this feature deliver?*

Managed Installer uses a new rule collection in AppLocker or Device Guard to specify one or more executables that are trusted by the organisation as an authorised source for application deployment, for example, the SSCM agent or a PowerShell Script.

Specifying an application as a managed installer will cause Windows to tag any files that are created from that application (or child processes it launches) as having originated from a trusted installation authority.

These tagged applications are then permitted to execute by the Application Control solution, as if they had been explicitly permitted by the whitelist, without requiring any configuration changes to be implemented and distributed to the users' endpoints.

### *What are the considerations for using this feature?*

This approach to configuring permitted applications is best suited to those environments where software installations are all managed through the software distribution platform. Any software installed outside of this managed installer mechanism (e.g. installed by a support engineer), will still need to be managed through normal Application Control configuration and will, therefore, be subject to its limitations.

Due to the nature of the managed installer option, users operating with admin accounts (or malware executing in the user's context) could abuse the capability to introduce unwanted applications into the endpoint environment, which would then be permitted to execute. As such it is not suitable for use in environments where users retain local administrative accounts.

Conversely, where application installations run the application at the end of the install process, any files created by the installed application will also be tagged and allowed to execute by the whitelist.

*What are the limitations of this feature?*

As Managed Installer utilises the concept of a "tag" to identify applications which have originated from the managed installer process, there are circumstances where these tags may be lost. This can be something as simple as applications which feature self-update mechanisms which overwrite the originally tagged application with a new version.

When the tag is lost, the application is then treated as any other unknown application and is blocked from executing. This would then require a configuration change in order to resolve and the associated challenges.

Similarly, modern applications or those installations which extract files first before executing are not supported by the feature and would again require manual configuration within the Application Control policy in order to support them.

## MICROSOFT APPLICATION CONTROL – WINDOWS DEFENDER APPLICATION CONTROL: CLOUD-DRIVEN EXECUTION CONTROL

*What is this feature?*

Microsoft has developed an Application Control capability driven by data in its cloud platform, as a means to address the same challenge as Managed Installer - namely supporting new applications without needing to update configurations. This technology is particularly useful for those organisations who have not adopted a software deployment technology such as Microsoft SCCM and may also suffer from more limited resources.

Microsoft targets this functionality towards the SMB market, but it may fit in any environments which are "lightly-managed" or where less mature application control processes exist. It can be configured to allow only Windows and Microsoft Store applications to run and to optionally allow any application which Microsoft's cloud data identifies as having a "good" reputation.

### What does this feature deliver?

This tool allows "known good" code identified by Microsoft Intelligent Security Graph (ISG) and automatically authorises application executables based upon positive reputation. It is also designed to complement corporately defined allow or deny rules and to work alongside Managed Installer.

It includes the ability to automatically re-validate reputation on system reboots to catch anything which may have changed since it was initially run. This allows changes to an application's reputation standing to be picked up

These can be managed from both SCCM and Intune (more on these and their respective considerations as management platforms later).

### What are the considerations for using this feature?

Implementing using the code integrity policies and trusting applications with good reputations provides a balance between security and usability and certainly offers a significant improvement when compared to an environment without any whitelisting controls in place.

However, the ISG allows for a very broad base of trusted applications, including many which are in good standing from a reputational standpoint, but which would not be wanted in an enterprise environment. A simple example might be widely used cloud-based file sharing tools provided by legitimate vendors, which may present data leakage risks or be prohibited by certain compliance mandates or legal restrictions.

### *What are the limitations of this feature?*

Using this approach to whitelisting applications means placing all of the control into Microsoft's hands, and whilst that may be an acceptable trade off for some organisations, particularly where they have no application control in place, this may allow undesirable applications to run.

### Summary

As previously stated, many of the tools available in Windows to implement application whitelisting have significant limitations, which ultimately means they are better suited to fixed function devices such as kiosk systems and ATMs that require few updates and settings changes and no admin users (or possibly no active users at all).

The end user experience is extremely limited, with yet more unintuitive messaging, no user support, and no ability to customise the messaging presented to the end user. The inference from Microsoft is that this will change in future releases.

Many are not compatible with BYOD (Bring Your Own Device) because of the reliance upon hardware features for certain aspects and because it would require the end user to consent to their device being taken over by the organisation.

The above design limitations will severely hinder the uptake of these technologies other than in situations where users do not interact with devices.

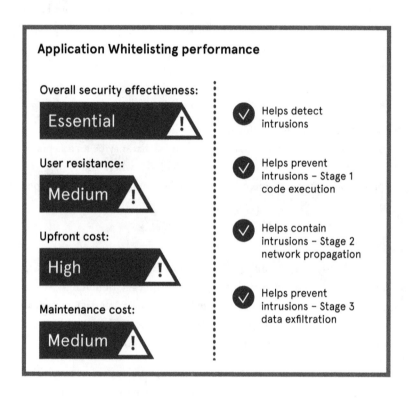

## 4.3. **Microsoft Security Technology**

Whilst many of Microsoft's client-side security technologies have traditionally been integrated directly into the operating system itself, the current trend is for these to be delivered by a tightly-integrated but logically separate product called "Windows Defender".

The Windows Defender brand now represents a far more diverse set of capabilities than the antivirus product which first bore the name in earlier versions of Windows. These capabilities provide a useful toolbox for organisations developing a defense-in-depth security model, but as we've already mentioned, there is no such thing a free lunch, and many of the more advanced features and capabilities are chargeable.

## WINDOWS DEFENDER – EXPLOIT GUARD

### *What is this feature?*

Windows Defender Exploit Guard (EG) is a collection of host intrusion protection capabilities introduced in Windows 10, allowing you to manage and reduce the attack surface of the applications used within your environment.

**Exploit Guard is comprised of several features, including:**

- Attack Surface Reduction (ASR)
- Controlled Folder Access (CFA)
- Network Protection (NP)
- Exploit Protection (EP)

With the exception of Exploit Protection, each of these features is dependent upon the real-time protection capability of the Windows Defendpoint Antivirus being enabled. They also require a licence for Microsoft's Windows Defender Advanced Threat Protection (ATP) for reporting in the Windows Defender ATP console.

## WINDOWS DEFENDER – EXPLOIT GUARD: ATTACK SURFACE REDUCTION (ASR)

Exploit protection automatically applies a number of exploit mitigation techniques on both the operating system processes and on individual apps, including many of the protections which were originally included in Microsoft's Enhanced Mitigation Experience Toolkit (EMET).

This includes historic mitigations for Return Orientated Programming (ROP) and enforcing mandatory Address Space Layout Randomisation (ASLR), as well as adding additional techniques including disabling Win32k system calls and implementing code integrity guard.

## WINDOWS DEFENDER – EXPLOIT GUARD: NETWORK PROTECTION (NP)

The Network Protection capability focuses on reducing the attack surface of your devices from Internet-based events. Unlike Windows Defender SmartScreen, whose protection is limited to Microsoft browsers (IE7-Edge), NP prevents any application on the endpoint from connecting to high-risk domains which might host phishing scams, exploits, and other malicious content.

Access restrictions to domains are driven by a reputation scoring system, which blocks the HTTP/HTTPS connection if a particular domain's reputation is defined as "low".

# WINDOWS DEFENDER – CONTROLLED FOLDER ACCESS (CFA)

Strongly focused on addressing the challenges of ransomware, Controlled Folder Access helps you protect valuable data from malicious apps and threats.

Applications (i.e. executables including .exe, .scr, .dll files and others) are evaluated by Windows Defender Antivirus, to determine whether they are malicious or safe. If the app is flagged as malicious or simply identified as suspicious, it will not be allowed to make changes to any files in a folder protected by CFA.

### *What are the considerations for using this feature?*

Microsoft states that "some security mitigation technologies may have compatibility issues with some applications", which requires that you perform extensive auditing and review prior to enforcing many of the available controls.

The implications of these incompatibilities are not limited to third party integrations or extensions to Microsoft products, but can impair or prevent Microsoft's own tools functioning normally or from interacting with one another. Simple tasks such as embedding an Excel spreadsheet within a Word document or PowerPoint presentation can be blocked, as well as third party security and productivity tools being impacted.

### *What are the limitations of this feature?*

Due to the nature of many of these controls and how they are enforced, the user may experience errors which are not user-friendly and are in some cases neither verbose or do not relate in any way to the controls being applied. This can cause confusion and frustration amongst users and may increase helpdesk call volumes as users seek to understand what is happening on their endpoint.

Additionally, as with many Microsoft security technologies, there is a significant lack of any capability to handle exceptions in a dynamic fashion (i.e. without resorting to configuration changes), and in many cases, there is no provision for creating exceptions to the defined control.

Where issues are encountered, there is limited configuration available to work around them, meaning that often it requires functionality to be turned off entirely, as they all too often interfere with users' ability to perform their role effectively (or potentially at all).

## 4.4. Management Tools

This section looks at the different management technologies offered to make central management of the endpoint easier. There is overlap between least privilege, application control and standard configuration topics in this section.

## GROUP POLICY – WHERE DOES THIS FIT IN?

### Deploying software with Group Policy

One area Group Policy can help with is the installation of software. This is often seen as one of the biggest challenges to implementing least privilege: If admin privileges are removed users have to rely on an administrator or a software distribution system to install or update applications. The Group Policy Software Installation system helps with this challenge as it allows for Group Policy objects to be targeted at the users and computers that require software to be installed.

However, its functionality is limited, and I would only recommend this for small and medium-sized businesses. For large enterprises, I would suggest using System Center Configuration Manager or another third party software distribution platform instead, as they offer more functionality. I will discuss this option later.

Group Policy Software Installation (GPSI) requires applications to be packaged in Windows Installer .msi format. This in itself is a problem, as many legacy applications rely on older setup technologies, which usually end with the .exe file extension and don't contain a .msi file. These types of installers are not supported by GPSI installation. Technically speaking, you have the option of creating a .zap package. However, this involves taking a snapshot of a machine before and after installation. In addition, the logged in user must be an administrator to complete the installation process. In practical terms, unless the application is packaged as a .msi, it is unlikely to be worth the effort.

## Deploying Software with Start-up scripts

When it is not practical to leverage Group Policy Software Installation for software deployment, such as legacy installers, a plausible option is to create a start-up or login script. These can be used to automate the installation routes and are deployable via Group Policy. Start-up scripts will run in the system context and would not need administrative accounts (and could introduce potentially dangerous mistakes), whereas login scripts run in the context of the logged in user. One thing to be aware of is these scripts can be complicated to create, test and manage, so they do not provide a quick deployment option and will most likely only be used for applications that many users need. GPSI deployment provides better lifecycle and awareness of the installation state.

*What are the limitations of this feature?*

In short, Group Policy functionality is limited and will only be useful in the smallest of organisations. In later sections, I will discuss the application of settings using Group Policy.

## Can Group Policy ensure the application of standardised configuration?

When it comes to configuring a large number of machines, Group Policy is a great and effective tool for ensuring a standard configuration across the estate. Group Policy is an infrastructure that allows you to implement specific configurations for users and computers. Settings are contained in Group Policy objects (GPOs), which are linked to the following Active Directory service containers: sites, domains, or organisational units (OUs). The settings within GPOs are then evaluated by the affected targets, using the hierarchical nature of Active Directory. Consequently, Group Policy is one of the top reasons for deploying Active Directory because it allows you to manage user and computer objects.

Many IT professionals incorrectly think Group Policy can be used to remove access to part of the system or settings. In fact, all you are doing is essentially "hiding" settings and options from the user. If the user has an administrative account, they can simply access the setting by finding the application and manually launching it or navigating to the registry and disabling Group Policy.

Another misconception amongst IT professionals is the belief that admin privileges can be assigned to applications via Group Policy. This is incorrect. You can manage group membership, giving people administrative accounts etc., but you cannot assign privileges to applications with GPOs. Permissions on files, folders and registry keys can be managed via GPOs, but this is distinctly different.

**Applying the below settings will help ensure standard configuration**

1. Set the system boot order to ensure boot is from the local hard disk

2. Prevent users from booting into another OS and tampering with system files by setting a BIOS password

3. Encrypt the system volume using BitLocker for the highest level of security

4. Use Application Control to block unknown applications from running

5. Assign users read-only mandatory user profiles so they cannot override settings

6. Configure Group Policy to reapply settings, even if the policy has not been changed since the last refresh

*What are the limitations of this feature?*

Group Policy is not completely watertight, and when running as an administrator, Group Policy (and other security controls) can be evaded in seconds. However, it is still possible to find your way around Group Policy even as a standard user. Windows applications are responsible for enforcing their own Group Policy settings. Standard users have full permissions over the processes they own, so there is the potential for one running process to modify another to ignore Group Policy. Therefore, you need to implement the correct configuration recommendations to help secure it, which are outlined below. However, as with most things, these settings result in a trade-off between usability and security or affect system performance.

*What are the considerations for using this feature?*

Developing configuration settings with good security properties is a complex task beyond the ability of individual users, requiring analysis of potentially hundreds or thousands of options in order to make good choices.

Even if a strong initial configuration is developed and installed, it must be continually managed to avoid security "decay" as software is updated or patched, new security vulnerabilities are reported, and configurations are "tweaked" to allow the installation of new software or the support of new operational requirements.

## SYSTEM CENTER CONFIGURATION MANAGER (SCCM)

System Center Configuration Manager (SCCM) is a systems management software product developed by Microsoft for managing large groups of computers running Windows, Windows Embedded, Mac OS X, Linux or UNIX, as well as various mobile operating systems such as Windows Phone, Symbian, iOS and Android. It provides remote control, patch management, software distribution, OS deployment, network access protection, and hardware and software inventory.

There have been many iterations of the solution, adding features such as the ability to manage SCCM configuration by AD site. I typically see software distribution, patch management and inventory management as the most widely used features. However, SCCM also includes technologies like its advance client feature, which is capable of dealing with distributed networks and remote clients that may not always connect back to the same SCCM service.

**Features provided by SCCM:**

1.  Windows management
2.  Application delivery

3.  Device management

4.  Virtual desktop management

5.  Endpoint Protection

6.  Compliance and settings management

7.  Software update management

8.  Power management

9.  Operating system deployment

10. Client health and monitoring

11. Asset intelligence

12. Inventory

13. Reporting

## Below are some of the key advantages of SCCM

### User-centric management

Software distributions can now be targeted at users rather than just at devices. This is especially useful where users share the same machine. A user's "primary device" can be defined (or logically worked out), and different software can be deployed to their primary devices vs other devices they use. For example, if a manager logs onto a subordinate's workstation temporarily, if the system is not designated as his primary device, any applications specifically targeted at the manager's primary device will not be available to him on that system.

### Configuration settings remediation

The ability to report and alert on compliance has been useful in monitoring and managing configuration drift. SCCM has the ability to remediate WMI, registry, and script settings that are not compliant. Automated remediation can drastically reduce the time that a non-compliant configuration stays out of compliance.

### Collection-based configuration settings

Client settings can be customised and targeted at specific collections of devices within the same site or different sites. Site hierarchies can also be built.

### Dependency-based software distribution

Requirement Rules and/or Global Conditions can be specified as preconditions for a deployment. Examples of this include available hardware (e.g., memory, available hard disk space, etc.), software prerequisites (e.g., Office must be installed as a prerequisite for Office SP1), and user affinity (Is this the user's primary device?). An application can have multiple deployment types (such as an upgrade, uninstall, virtual app, local install, mobile device version) and the deployment type can be triggered based on the Requirement Rules or Global Conditions.

### Software Center and Application Catalogue

Users can be given the ability to set some configurable settings as well as request and install available applications. This "App Store" model can minimise some of the challenges associated with managing devices and applications for mobile technology-savvy users that need more flexibility.

### *What are the considerations for using this feature?*

I have seen organisations have some great success with SCCM when it comes to OS deployment, patch management and the deployment of sanctioned line of business applications. Where it does less well is in the ability to deal with flexible on-demand installations/changes. What I mean by this is the ability to quickly deploy software or configuration changes, which only a handful of users need, as the packaging, testing and deployment overheads are too large to be cost-effective.

This results in users being given administrative accounts to install and make system updatesor changes, or the IT team completing the activity on the user's behalf. Even with the more flexible features SCCM brings, IT teams still need to configure and deploy these features, and it is often the case that end-user demand does not have the luxury of time.

As more of the workforce becomes mobile (base from home) or employees are on temporary contracts, organisations are now faced with another challenge, namely' How do we manage loosely connected devices?' These devices will not have an SCCM agent installed and may never be part of the corporate domain. To help answer this, Microsoft has introduced the concept of Modern Management (see the section on this topic)

# SYSTEM IMAGES – OS AND SOFTWARE DISTRIBUTION

Enterprises will typically utilise imaging technologies, such as Microsoft Deployment Toolkit (MDT) or similar, to pre-configure the OS and applications, then deploy them over the network from a dedicated server. Organisations that can afford the necessary infrastructure and have the required skills can leverage this technology to resolve some of the problems associated with deploying software to users running with Least Privilege.

Covering all the different technology aspects of this topic is beyond the scope of this book. The main reason is that technology in this area moves on very fast. For example, in an early version of Windows, images had to be built for specific hardware configurations. But as technology has moved on, images are now more flexible and have become more of a collection of configuration options and software that will be deployed to a machine.

*What are the considerations for using this feature?*

Many organisations combine imaging and other management systems for maximum flexibility. Most enterprises are now moving to a lighter image with more control being applied via SCCM or other tools. Images still have a place and can offer more speed when systems are identical - such as Point of Sales systems - and can help deploy an OS with a good starting point, but they do little to maintain the build over time or provide the user with flexibility. However, in a dynamic desktop environment, a lighter touch approach is required. As discussed earlier, they also don't help in remote workforce situations.. This topic is discussed in more detail in the Modern Management section.

## WINDOWS MODERN MANAGEMENT

*What is this feature?*

As you have seen throughout this book, the task of deploying an Operating System and its associated applications requires IT professionals to do lots of manual and time-consuming tasks to maintain company-owned infrastructure and devices. With the rise in workforce flexibility and advances in cloud technology, the demand for more automation and a lighter touch approach has arisen.

With the introduction of Windows 10, Microsoft has attempted to simplify the deployment and management with Enterprise Mobility Management (EMM) solutions, which it is collectively calling Modern Management. With modern management, you can now manage company-owned Windows 10 devices of all kinds, from desktop PCs to HoloLens and Surface Hubs.

Microsoft defines modern management as an approach of managing Windows 10 to simplify deployment and management (creating nimble

IT operations in the process), improve security, provide a better end-user experience, and lower costs for Windows devices. Microsoft views this as the evolution of IT. The traditional way ("old world") of deploying the Microsoft Windows operating system is to leverage Active Directory, Group Policy and System Center Configuration Manager for desktops and a Mobile Device Management (MDM) solution for deploying across mobile devices.

Microsoft aims to bring this MDM experience to the desktop world – allowing for desktops and mobile devices to be deployed and managed in a single, unified approach. The "new world" way of deployment and management ("modern management") is through the cloud. Specifically, it is done with what Microsoft calls Enterprise Mobility and Security (EMS), which is comprised of Azure Active Directory, Microsoft InTune, and Azure Information Protection. Windows AutoPilot, which is deeply integrated with Azure AD and Intune, simplifies and personalises the out-of-the-box experience for users, joins the device to Azure AD, and enrols it to Intune. Users' email, apps, files and preferences, as well the organisation's security settings, are also automatically applied by Intune without the need to create custom OS wwimages.

Microsoft's vision for Modern Management depicts a scenario where an employee orders their devices direct from the manufacturer, who then ships them directly to the end-user. The end-user powers up the devices, enters an Azure-AD account, and the device is provisioned via InTune. IT staff do not need to re-image the devices or even touch them, significantly reducing costs. Microsoft also envisions a "no software" world, where business applications like Office 365 are accessed through the cloud and the Windows Store for Business. This is a great vision, but is it a reality?

### *What are the considerations of this feature?*

Microsoft is providing these features to keep up with the pace of change. Consumers are demanding simpler and superior experiences when using enterprise software, and as a result, Microsoft customers are demanding solutions to meet these needs. Microsoft is also facing the reality of the industry: almost every major software vendor is transitioning to the cloud (or creating a complementary cloud offering), as this better meets the needs of consumers and saves IT resources (e.g. infrastructure costs, management costs, etc.).

However, most Microsoft customers are still in the traditional ("old world") mode of deploying operating systems such as Windows. While they may have moved to the cloud for other solutions (particularly business applications), infrastructure solutions such as OS deployments are behind the curve. Some early adopters have embraced the cloud for OS deployment - or modern management - but these have tended to be smaller, more agile organisations that don't have to support legacy applications developed many years ago. While adoption of modern management is expected to grow as more organisations adopt Windows 10, mass adoption is likely many years away as organisations both upgrade operating systems and decide if modern management is viable.

With this in mind, Microsoft has provided co-management option that allows Windows to be managed by traditional technologies (AD, Group Policy and SCCM) and Azure AD and Intune. Thus, allowing for a transition.

### *What are the limitations of this feature?*

A huge consideration for most medium to large enterprises is the sheer number of legacy applications that were developed many years ago and the hundreds of configuration options applied to there operating systems and applications. For example, Internet Explorer has ~1500 Group Policy options that can be applied. The Modern Management approach only provides a fraction of settings leaving many organisations without the ability to apply the controls they need. At present InTune is designed for a very light touch configuration which will suffice for an organisation not looking to apply corporate controls to their machines. While Microsoft has painted a vision and roadmap for enterprises to transition to a cloud-based modern management approach, they have not enabled a complete solution. Many organisation while requiring more management configuration options.

While Microsoft has improved security in Windows 10, it still is insufficient for the needs of complex enterprises that must deal with an ever-changing landscape of cybersecurity threats. A modern management approach makes it easier to deploy and manage Windows 10 for remote, off-the-network employees, but does not address the need for these remote workers to easily install essential applications in a manner that balances the security needs of the company and the user-friendly experience they expect.

If IT staff cannot as quickly provide support to remote workers, for example, these users will need to be provided with the ability to "self-manage" their devices. Users will need to install applications and configure their own devices. As Intune cannot configure many of the settings centrally, users will need to do it themselves and therefore need a local admin account. But if the user is given a local admin account, this will allow for unauthorised applications to be installed on endpoints, exposing the business to costly and devastating cyber attacks.

Modern management may make the deployment of an OS and cloud apps easier, but it does nothing to reduce the attack surface on the endpoint, and in many ways makes it worse.

## 4.5. Patching – typical tools and tech
. . . . . . . . . . . . . . . . . . . . . . . . . . . . . . . . . . . . . . . . .

As discussed, patching is the best way to fix code vulnerabilities and stop the weaponisation of code flaws. However, it is not easy to stay up to date. Below are some of the ways this is made easier.

### WINDOWS SERVER UPDATE SERVICES (WSUS)

Windows Server Update Services (WSUS) is a Microsoft tool that allows administrators to manage the distribution of updates and hotfixes released for Microsoft products to computers in a corporate environment. WSUS downloads these updates from the Microsoft Update website and then distributes them to computers on a network. WSUS runs on Windows Server and is free to licensed Microsoft customers. It includes many benefits, including download optimisation and central control of updates and patches.

### USING SYSTEM CENTER CONFIGURATION MANAGER TO STAY UP TO DATE

System Center Configuration Manager provides features that offer more flexibility and control over the complex task of applying software updates to endpoints in an enterprise.

SCCM includes features which allow general maintenance windows and a different maintenance window for software updates. Software updates will only be installed during the "update window" and new software during the "general" windows, thus giving you more control.

The two main ways to deploy updates are Manual and Automatic. In Manual deployment, a set of software updates are selected and deployed to collections. Automatic updates are configured using automatic deployment rules. This method is used for deploying updates on a schedule. Rules can be created to defined the type of updates to implement (for example, all security software updates released in the last week).

SCCM leverages WSUS, so think of it as a more granular way of deploying updates with better targeting.

# WINDOWS UPDATE FOR BUSINESS

With the demand for more flexible working environments, Windows 10 has seen the introduction of Windows Update for Business. Combined with Intune, organisations can manage devices that are not joined to a domain or are joined to Microsoft Azure Active Directory (Azure AD). Group Policy or MDM solutions such as Intune can be used to configure the settings that control how and when Windows 10 devices are updated. This is provided as a free service.

**Features provided[24]:**

- Co-exists with domain joined machines
- The creation of deployme rings, where administrators can specify which devices go first in an update wave, and which ones will come later (to ensure any quality bars are met).
- Ability including or excluding drivers as part of Microsoft-provided updates

---

24 https://docs.microsoft.com/en-us/windows/deployment/update/waas-manage-updates-wufb

- Integration with existing management tools such as Windows Server Update Services (WSUS), System Center Configuration Manager, and Microsoft Intune.

- Peer-to-peer delivery for Microsoft updates, which optimises bandwidth efficiency and reduces the need for an on-site server caching solution.

- Control over diagnostic data level to provide reporting and insights in Windows Analytics.

## THIRD PARTY CLOUD UPDATE SERVICES

There are many SasS based patch management solutions that offer the same functionality as Microsoft's technologies, with the added benefit of supporting updates for non-Microsoft tools and providing better support for remote disconnected users (users who do not connect to the domain or come into the office). Below are some pros and cons to this approach:

**Pros**

- Does not require remote users to connect to VPNs
- Better reporting analytics
- More granular control
- Other capabilities include software deployment over the air
- Supports Windows and Mac (InTune does not)
- Caters for third party application patching
- Cons
- Could potentially pause scans/updates and therefore be out of date quicker
- Doesn't support 'feature updates' (too risky re-installing the OS over the air)

I have seen many organisations adopt a hybrid approach where they use native windows functionally for OS upgrades and cloud services for everything else.

## Summary - Find a way to stay up to date!

Understanding and managing vulnerabilities requires significant time, attention, and resources. Some automated patching tools may not detect or install certain patches. If installed on a per-user basis, patches need to be re-downloaded per user, wasting time and hard drive space. What's more, on its own, it is unable to track, trace and destroy attacks. There have been negative reports that patches cause systems not to boot. Also, they are unable to prevent attacks to applications and the system at large.

## Privilege management performance

Overall security effectiveness:

Essential

User resistance:

Medium

Upfront cost:

Medium

Maintenance cost:

Low

✓ Helps detect intrusions

? Helps prevent intrusions – Stage 1 code execution

✓ Helps contain intrusions – Stage 2 network propagation

✕ Helps prevent intrusions – Stage 3 data exfiltration

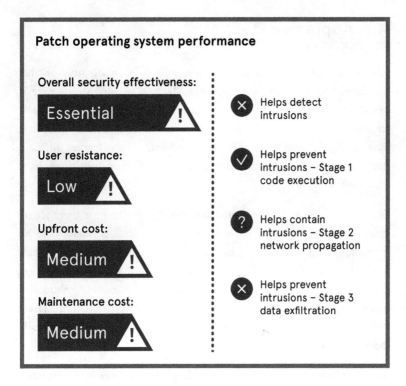

**Patch operating system performance**

Overall security effectiveness:

Essential ⚠️

User resistance:

Low ⚠️

Upfront cost:

Medium ⚠️

Maintenance cost:

Medium ⚠️

❌ Helps detect intrusions

✅ Helps prevent intrusions – Stage 1 code execution

❓ Helps contain intrusions – Stage 2 network propagation

❌ Helps prevent intrusions – Stage 3 data exfiltration

Another issue to take into account is the vast array of software used at organisations. Third party applications will not be managed by automation tools like WSUS, meaning you will need to track and manage updates manually. The problem is compounded when you do not have application control, as users introduce threats all the time, increasing the attack surface. If you mostly use Microsoft technologies, I have seen success by using a combination of cloud and on-premise Microsoft technologies to manage patches.

## 4.6. **Apple macOS**

Due to the pervasiveness of Windows, I have focused mainly on that platform. However, the use of Apple Macs as an enterprise device is on the rise and can't be ignored. The first, and perhaps the biggest challenge, is that macOS devices have not been designed for enterprises and in particular for enterprise management. They feature little in the way of centralised control capabilities, which we see throughout Microsoft's technologies.

For a long time, there has been a perception that Macs are more secure than Windows devices. However, their popularity has made them an increasing target for cybercriminals, with a growing number of threats now focusing on the platform. Whilst it is true that Apple devices are not susceptible to Windows malware, there are increasing volumes of macOS specific malware, which means users and system administrators must now implement effective security controls which have traditionally been deemed as unnecessary.

XCode Ghost Malware is one example of this and saw cybercriminals planting malware on Apple apps. Moreover, another Apple-specific threat is the KeRanger malware, which was hidden inside the installer of the popular Transmission BitTorrent client for OS X. Those unlucky enough to fall victim to it are also hit with a one Bitcoin (around $6,500 as of October 2018) ransom demand.

Apple even released High Sierra (macOS 10.13) with a bug which allowed anyone to log onto the device with "root" privileges using a blank password! This is a basic bug that should have been spotted early on in the testing stages of the most immature software, let alone in the operating system of a tech giant like Apple. It serves as a harsh reminder to users that they cannot rely on inbuilt security or a brand name alone.

Research carried out by JAMF suggests Mac usage is increasing in many organisations. It found that given a choice, 72 per cent of employees would favour a Mac over a PC and, as more than half of organisations (52 per cent) now allow workers to choose what kind of device they use, opre IT departments may have to take Macs into consideration[25].

The problem with this rise in usage is that until recently, there has been no viable solution for controlling and managing enterprise Macs. Historically, this meant Mac users were allowed privileges (such as full admin accounts) and the devices have generally been allowed to exist outside of the corporate network. As the popularity of Macs increases, so too do the risks. Symantec research revealed that in 2018, it saw an 80 per cent increase in the amount of new Mac malware[26] compared with the previous year.

## Don't treat Macs differently

Until recently, Mac security options have been behind the curve, and wholly reliant on detection.

One of the critical challenges for Mac users is that removing admin accounts makes it difficult to complete many everyday tasks (such as changing the time or installing a new printer) that you would expect them to be able to. On the Windows platform, provisioning all your users with admin account is unthinkable, but when it comes to Macs organisations often 'think different'.

Many senior executives in organisations have Macs, and the irony is that they are the least managed, least secure devices with the most access to data. This makes them a tempting candidate for criminals to target specifically.

---

25    https://www.jamf.com/resources/press-releases/jamf-survey-employees-are-more-
      productive-and-happier-when-they-choose-their-work-device/
26    https://www.symantec.com/content/dam/symantec/docs/reports/istr-23-executive-
      summary-en.pdf

The message then is clear - when it comes to security, treat Macs equally. The right approach is to follow the same best practice – patching, least privilege and whitelisting applications - on all devices, no matter what operating system is in use.

**Key Stats**

- **96%** of businesses now support Macs
- **66%** have workers that use Macs
- **98%** of Fortune 500 companies use Apple products
- **75%** of IT admins say that Macs do not offer increased security advantages
- **82%** of enterprise Mac users are not getting security updates
- **50%** say they are not ready to manage Macs
- **40%** of CIOs say they now have less confidence in Mac security.
- Sadly, **28%** still believe OS X is 'more secure' than Windows.

 **Macs should not be viewed as more secure than Windows endpoints**

The below sections detail the specific technologies that exist within the macOS.

# APPLE MACOS PRIVILEGE MANAGEMENT – PRIVILEGED USERS/GROUPS

### What is this feature?

As with other OsS such as Windows, macOS includes a small number of built-in groups to simplify assigning privileges and permissions, enabling users to be added to those groups and to inherit the capabilities assigned to them.

The environment also includes the famous, highly-privileged default user, 'root', who owns many of the system processes and has complete access to the macOS filesystem. However, this account is typically disabled by default after the installation of the OS is complete.

The recommendation is that the root account is never enabled, but where root's powers are required, they may be invoked by using a command 'sudo', which is described later in this chapter.

### What does this feature deliver?

Under a default macOS deployment, a user may be made a member of one of a number of local groups, which confer additional rights or privileges. By default, these are:

- Wheel
- Admin
- Developer

In earlier versions of macOS (prior to 10.3), the wheel group was used to grant users the right to become root by using the 'su' utility. However this has now been replaced by the admin group.

The admin group is used in place of the root user and grants users the right to perform almost all of the functions of 'root'. One different (and arguably advantage) of using the admin group, is that the privileges it confers can be used in the Finder GUI, rather than being limited to the Terminal command-line interface.

The exception to the capabilities of the admin group is that they cannot directly add, modify or remove files which are in the system domain, although they can use additional installer or software updater tools to perform these actions.

The developer group allows software developers working with Apple's Xcode and other developer tools to authorise developer privilege use, when debugging the applications they are developing, or when using performance tools. A member of the admin account can also provide this authorisation, but granting developer users membership of that group also confers the additional capabilities described above.

### *What are the considerations for using this feature?*

As noted earlier, Apple devices have not been architected with enterprise environments in mind. This presents challenges when needing to provision group memberships to multiple users and across multiple devices.

Without integrating into an environment such as Microsoft Active Directory to create shared and centralised identities (and having users log on with domain credentials to their Apple endpoint), users must be explicitly added to groups across each of the endpoints.

Using explicitly defined entries also mean these changes would have to be manually removed from each affected endpoint. Whereas, if domain security groups were used and nested within the local groups, privileges could be automatically revised as a users' group membership changed at the domain level, removing the need to change the endpoint directly.

*What are the limitations of this feature?*

The default groups lack any level of granular control over how users may utilise the privileges they are granted and cannot tailor the capabilities to specific circumstances or requirements. Whilst the developer group does provide a more specific set of privileges, unlike the admin group, ultimately the user may receive more privileges than they require to perform their role and expose the endpoint and organisation to undue risk.

There are also considerations around how some of the groups confer capabilities. In particular, some are usable in all interfaces, whilst others may only be used from the command-line. This may limit the ability for some users to utilise these privileges as part of performing the tasks they need to use those privileges for.

## APPLE MACOS PRIVILEGE MANAGEMENT – SECURITY SCHEMES (PERMISSIONS)

*What is this feature?*

The macOS environment includes a number of different security schemes to control access to files and folders, which are layered together to determine access to, and use of, them. These include:

- UNIX (BSD) Permissions
- POSIX access control lists (ACLs), and
- Sandbox Entitlements

These permissions may be used to grant users access to specific files and folders, including delegating access to standard users for paths or files which would be prevented by default.

### What does this feature deliver?

These permissions allow both broad and fine-grained control of who can access, use and modify objects in the macOS filesystem. This includes content files, as well as system binaries and other components.

Unix permissions enable the definition of a user or group as the owner of a file or folder, as well as the ownership setting for everyone else. This setting is broken into three tiers, owner, group and everyone and provides the basis for file permissions.

By default, the owner is automatically set to whoever created a file or introduced the object to the filesystem (e.g. copied or downloaded). For many of the system components, resources and applications, the root user is almost always the owner.

Also set by default, the group is inherited from the folder the object is created within. It is common for many objects to belong to the staff, wheel, or admin groups discussed previously. The intent of the Group ownership is to permit users other than the owner to access an object.

The everyone setting, perhaps as the name suggests, is used to define access for anyone (and everyone) who is not the object's owner, and who isn't part of the object's group.

This ownership setting provides a coarse-grained control over objects, whilst access control lists were layered on top, to provide more granular controls – these are often referred to as POSIX-style ACLs or permissions. They allow you to define privilege rules separately at each of the ownership tiers described previously.

In other words, the owner, the group, and everyone else has individually specified access to each file or folder. Further, because of the inherent hierarchy built into the file system, where folders can reside inside of other folders, you easily create a complex file structure that allows for varying levels of sharing and security.

Access control lists (ACLs) are not standardised across operating systems. However, Apple has adopted an implementation which is very similar to Microsoft's equivalent in NTFS. Its highly- flexible, but at the same time increases complexity thanks to several unique privilege and inheritance attribute types.

### What are the considerations for using this feature?

Apple attempts to insulate users from the complexities of the permissions controls available, limiting the options which can be set using the Finder interface to only the most common configurations. This enforces the use of command line tools in order to manage more complex settings combinations, which can give rise to errors.

Additionally, it is worth noting that where an ACL rule applies to a user or group, this configuration will override the traditional UNIX permissions. However, any users or groups that aren't the target of a specific ACL will still be in scope for the UNIX permissions in place.

### What are the limitations of this feature?

Historically, only a file or folder's owner could change its ownership or permissions, but now every administrator has the same capability.

You may observe many folders which are owned by root within a macOS filesystem, but which permit the admin user group to modify them, through this setting.

Much as we see with the Windows platform, the freedoms afforded to administrative and highly privileged users can be used to undermine the integrity of the controls being enforced, by authorising admin users to perform operations against.

## APPLE MACOS PRIVILEGE MANAGEMENT – SUDO

### *What is this feature?*

Sudo is a command-line utility (program) provided as part of the macOS environment to assist in supporting a least privilege environment. It is provided as a means to invoke a command using another user account, typically one with greater privileges than those assigned to the logged-on user. However, it should not be confused with the 'su' command, which allows users to switch to another user, but requires you to know the credentials of that user.

Whilst Sudo was historically a contraction of "superuser do", as it allowed users to invoke a command as 'superuser', its capabilities have now extended to support other accounts, and so sudo is now taken to mean "substitute user and do".

### *What does this feature deliver?*

The sudo command allows a user to invoke a command by issuing the sudo command ahead of any other commands they wish to perform, for example: "sudo shutdown."

By default, users are then asked to re-authenticate themselves within the console interface, and their requested command is then compared to a sudoers configuration file. If the command is found in the sudoers file for that user, it is executed. However, if it is not found, it can be audited to provide a record of the attempted usage.

### What are the considerations for using this feature?

In order to allow a user to invoke a command as root (or any other user), you must first define them (the user and command) within the sudoers configuration file. The file may also be used to define very broad access, or more granularly dictate what commands a user may execute with those elevated rights.

The sudoers file is edited by hand and may contain a mixture of aliases which may be used to represent groups of users, groups of hosts and commands. However, the most important is the user specifications, which define what commands a user may run elevated through a combination of parameters:

```
<user list> <host list> = <operator list> <tag list> <command list>
```

When invoking sudo, it is possible to use a number of parameters to suppress further requests for user credentials. By default you are prompted every 15 minutes, regardless of how many commands you issue.

### What are the limitations of this feature?

As with other tools to assist with the management of privileges, the sudo command can only be invoked from the command line, which may limit its usability for broader user groups. It can also require knowledge of the specific command or tool (and its own syntax) in order to use them.

This required knowledge and the need to manually configure typically leads to users being granted overly permissive access and in many cases, the ability to run any command elevated, against the intention of the capability and what good practice dictates.

The sudoers file is extremely sensitive to syntax and formatting errors, which is why "visudo" is recommended as the only way to modify the file. The challenges of the syntax and the required understanding of the commands users require often leads to misconfiguration, but also increases the size and complexity of the file and its management as you attempt to grant more specific/granular privileges to specific users or groups.

## APPLE MACOS - APPLICATION CONTROL

Limiting which applications can execute is clearly a highly effective control. However Apple's method is somewhat different, forgoing the type of application control approaches adopted by Microsoft which puts the organisation and user in control.

Using the same model applied to its iOS phone/tablet environment, Apple prefers to retain control and visibility of the macOS environment through the use of the Apple App Store, as well as some complementary malware protection capabilities, so the firm is able to blacklist applications when required.

Apple was the first to offer a curated application store where users can browse, download and install software. Developers who wish to distribute their software through the App Store must get a Developer ID from Apple and submit their applications for review before they can ultimately be made available through the store.

This curation process is intended to ensure that applications within the store are safe for users to install and use and comply with all of Apple's development guidelines. Applications are digitally signed by the developer, using an Apple-issued code signing certificate, given Apple the power to respond should applications, and their developers misbehave.

However, this is not the only way applications are made available to macOS, with some third-party applications being distributed outside of the store. This is because their applications do not conform to the design guidelines for App Store apps, Apple's development guidelines, or they need to function in a way not possible for a store application.

This can include many security products, due to the way technologies such as antivirus need to operate, but also includes developer and design tools and even Microsoft Office (although Office apps are also available from the App Store too).

Control of these types of applications is largely beyond the scope of the native tools, aside from the GateKeeper control discussed below, with more granular and restrictive controls requiring third party solutions.

# APPLE MACOS APPLICATION CONTROL – GATEKEEPER

*What is this feature?*

Introduced in the Mountain Lion OS X release, Gatekeeper is one of several controls within the macOS environment designed to protect against malware and unwanted applications broadly, by providing system administrators with a means to limit the applications a user may install.

*What does this feature deliver?*

The GateKeeper control is exposed as a radio button which allows system administrators to determine whether users are permitted to install applications solely from the App Store, or from the App Store and from "identified developers", which are those who have a developer ID and signing certificate issued by Apple.

If you are having trouble locating the control, rather confusingly it is not labelled as 'GateKeeper' anywhere in the UI. It is found in the General tab of the "Security & Privacy" system preference pane in macOS, under the heading "Allow apps downloaded from:".

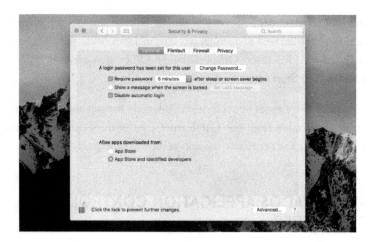

Under a default macOS installation, this setting will default to allow only applications from the Apple App Store applications to be installed. Attempting to change this setting does require administrative privileges, so by default, it offers a level of protection to users operating with standard user account.

However, it should be noted that Apple has made a fairly significant security compromise to this feature, in order to minimise the end user impact, which is described in the limitations section below.

### What are the considerations for using this feature?

Whilst this setting by default offers a level of protection for the end-user, for many enterprise users with a macOS device, these controls can impact their ability to work effectively by prompting them when running certain applications, which can become increasingly frustrating.

Similarly, when a single user in a team is affected by a GateKeeper restriction, there are no means to resolve that on behalf of other users (although an individual user won't be repeatedly prompted about the same application), requiring each user to perform the same workaround steps.

Enterprise administrators are limited in their ability to dynamically change these settings to meet the different requirements of individual user communities, particularly those who may need to regularly interact with (install or use) software from developers who are not "identified developers."

### What are the limitations of this feature?

When operating with full administrative accounts, users can alter the GateKeeper configuration setting also to allow software from identified developers.

Whilst this change does not significantly increase the risk the user is exposed to, as these developers will have at least been approved by Apple, the user may also use that same privilege to execute a command (sudo spctl –master-disable) to allow them to expose a third setting which was hidden by default in the macOS Sierra release.

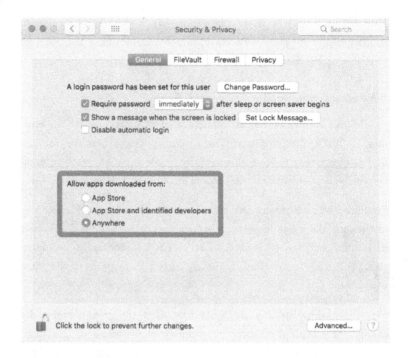

The "Anywhere" setting disables GateKeeper and prevents it from displaying any prompts to end-users and from blocking the execution apps from any publishers (whether they are known/trusted by Apple or not) or unsigned apps.

However, the most significant consideration is that even when configured in the default "App Store" only mode, users will be prompted when attempting to launch an app from an unidentified developer. However, they can Control-Click (right-click) on the app and select 'Open', which will prompt the user again, but ultimately allow the user to continue to launch the app.

Whilst this does not grant the application any additional privileges, if the user is running with an administrative account, a malicious application could leverage their elevated privileges as part of their attack. Even standard user account may be sufficient for attacks such as Ransomware.

## Summary

Gaining control of Macs within your enterprise is essential and possible. Traditional problems, such as a lack of visibility on activity and user behaviour, and the need for admin accounts, can be overcome even with standard accounts issued instead of full admin accounts.

Look for solutions that allow for specific privileges to be assigned based on the user's day-to-day needs, as well as enterprise ready application control. This provides users with the flexibility they need to get the job done and means organisations can secure all endpoints. Take a look at your workplace. Windows may remain the dominant platform, but if Macs are in use, the time to secure them is now.

# 4.7. Summary – The path of least resistance

As you can see, there is a lot to get right. There is always some external pressure applied to IT departments, which results in corners being cut and leads to an increased attack surface. If there was an infinite amount of resource and time, these tools could be combined to solve the problem. Unfortunately, we all know that is not the case.

PART TWO

# Technology to achieve defence in depth

CHAPTER 5

# Protection that works

The key to any security posture should be a proactive Defence in Depth (DiD) strategy. No security solution offers 100 per cent protection, so you need to have a multi-layered approach to tackle modern threats and remain relevant in a constantly evolving landscape. This is DiD and to do it effectively, you need to prioritise key strategies - such as Patching, Privilege Management and Application Whitelisting - and place them at the heart of your security design.

Done right, DiD can actually yield results extremely quickly and in many cases 'overnight'. Layering multiple strategies makes initial penetration much harder for attackers, both externally and internally, and reduces the potential for privilege escalation if an account is compromised. The temptation exists for IT and security professionals to deploy the easiest and most familiar technologies first. However, in the modern age of cyber threats, this is not the most effective use of resources, so businesses should invest in those measures proven to provide the most control against the riskiest threat vectors.

The DiD strategy I am proposing here is not based on detection or blacklists, but looks at practical ways to deliver the security foundations discussed in chapter 2. I will explain how security and freedom can be achieved by layering technologies that can actually be implemented. Later, in chapter 7, I will delve into specifics on how these technologies can be configured.

# 5.1. **How Defence in Depth works**

In 2011 Lockheed-Martin worked on a framework to describe the intrusion kill chain or model to defend computer networks. This has widely been adopted as the de facto standard used to describe cyber attacks and has been adapted many times. The basis of this work described attacks occurring in stages and that the opportunity exists to disrupt attacks at each of these stages, in a Defense in Depth approach. It can also be used as a tool to apply continuous improvement to your defences.

The framework describes threats progressing through several stages:[27]

1. **Reconnaissance:** Intruder selects a target, researches it, and attempts to identify vulnerabilities in the target network.

2. **Weaponisation:** Intruder creates remote access malware weapon, such as a virus or worm, tailored to one or more vulnerabilities.

---

27    https://en.wikipedia.org/wiki/Kill_chain

3. **Delivery:** Intruder transmits weapon to target (e.g., via e-mail attachments, websites or USB drives)**Exploitation:** Malware weapon's program code triggers, which takes action on target network to exploit the vulnerability.

4. **Installation:** Malware weapon installs access point (e.g., "backdoor") usable by an intruder.

5. **Command and Control:** Malware enables an intruder to have "hands on the keyboard" - persistent access to the target network.

6. **Actions on Objective:** Intruder takes action to achieve their goals, such as data exfiltration, data destruction, or encryption for ransom.

If we look at the above in the context of Defence in Depth technologies we highlighted in chapter 2, we can see that most of the attack stage would be thwarted by implementing those technologies. For example:

- **Stage 2** - Weaponisation : Would be stopped by up to date patching.
- **Stage 3** - Delivery and Stage 4 - Exploitation: Would be prevented by application whitelisting.
- **Stage 5** - Installation and Stage 6 - Command and Control: Can be mitigated by least privilege.
- **Stage 7** - Actions on Objective: This stage would not be reached when using a DiD approach.

Admittedly, I am taking an oversimplified view of the world in the above example. However, the point holds true that in so many cases, cyber attacks can be stopped if the approaches described here are implemented correctly. Nothing is 100 per cent, but if you follow the advice in this book, you will significantly reduce your exposure.

The following diagram describes the specific attack vectors that are mitigated by the four approaches discussed in this chapter. More on this later.

# How defence in depth works

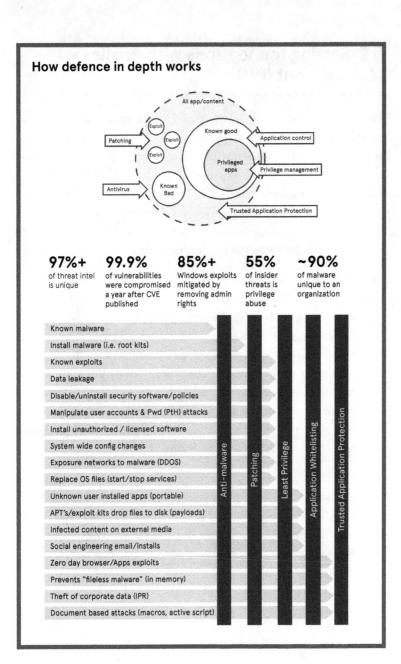

## 5.2. **Setting foundations with Privilege Management (PM)**

• • • • • • • • • • • • • • • • • • • • • • • • • • • • • • • • • • • • • • • •

We know that reducing administrative accounts is the single most effective thing you can do to reduce the Windows attack vector, mitigating the risk posed by 85 per cent of critical vulnerabilities reported by Microsoft[28]. The use of standard accounts instead of administrative accounts immediately increases your security protection, giving malware nowhere to go. Without the administrative accounts it seeks, these threats cannot reach the core network, where they cause the most damage or gain access to your corporate data.

To do this, you will need to implement Privilege Management (PM) technology that allows you to remove administrative accounts and deal with the challenges of standard accounts. This must have the capability to assign privileges directly to applications, tasks, scripts and installers rather than to users (importantly this must work for both desktops and servers) in order to be successful. This means you can allow all users to run with standard user accounts, protecting the operating system from internal and external threats that seek to exploit administrative accounts. However, your users still have the flexibility they need to be productive in their job roles, as discussed in chapter 3.

Typically, you need to consider operating system functions and line of business changes that are security sensitive or not required for the user's role. These will need to be defined in the PM solution and configured to be blocked or gated. Many solutions also offer the ability to detect which elevated privileges are being requested and will decide whether to allow the elevation.

---

28   www.avecto.com – see Microsoft Vulnerabilities report

**Example use cases**

- A security engineer needs access to manage the server's firewall configuration. They are granted privileged access to the Windows firewall control panel, as well as the ability to restart only the Windows firewall service.

- A developer requires admin privileges to compile the code and update the development environment.

- External consultants need access to manage the configuration solutions they provide. Privileges will only be granted to the applications and services they require.

- An employee within the account team needs to install a monthly update to their account application.

- A junior sysadmin needs access to perform some low-level maintenance tasks, such as check/clear event logs, defragment and cleanup disks. Administrative accounts for these specific tasks are granted during out-of-hours only.

- Remote workers require administrator privileges to install and configure peripherals.

- A senior sysadmin needs to diagnose a server outage and requires access to the server to diagnose the issue. A flexible 'on demand' policy is required to allow the sysadmin privileged and audited access to core Windows' debugging tools.

 Tip: Many PM solutions come with pre-defined definitions. Look for solutions that provide this rather than having to "reinvent the wheel".

In addition, by removing administrative accounts, you can maintain the integrity of your endpoint build/configuration (often referred to as the

"Gold Standard" build) by first securing it. Standard users do not have the power to change it. Users will then require a granular and flexible policy overlaid, which allows specific and detailed changes to be made. It is possible to strike this balance by using a Privilege Management technology, and I will be showing you how.

## Attack Vectors Mitigated by Least Privilege

As previously discussed, removing administrative accounts is the single biggest thing you can do to secure your endpoints. It mitigates 85 per cent of the security vulnerabilities in Microsoft technologies and is backed up by a number of industry studies. I have compiled a list of the attack vectors mitigated by the removal of administrative accounts to help paint the picture of its importance.

- Install spyware and adware
- Install kernel-mode rootkits
- Install system-level level keyloggers
- Install ActiveX controls, including IE and Explorer extensions
- Install and start services
- Stop existing services (such as the firewall)
- Access data belonging to other users
- Replace OS and other program files with Trojan horses
- Disable/uninstall anti-virus
- Create and modify user accounts
- Reset local passwords
- Pass the Hash (PtH) attacks
- Render the machine unbootable
- Exposure of entire networks to malware, viruses, and denial-of-service (DOS) attacks
- Data corruption or manipulation

- System-wide configuration changes
- Leakage of sensitive data
- System access and malware embedding in the OS
- Disabling security features/products
- Hiding files from the user
- Installing drivers and services
- System-wide persistence (HKLM run keys etc.)
- Disabling administrator applied policy
- Access other users files
- Malware exploiting administrative account
- UAC bypass attempts
- Malware installing outside of user profile

In addition, the majority of insider threats are related to privilege abuse. Privilege Management prevents users from covering their tracks or abusing the system as much.

## 5.3. Focus on secure, standard configuration
. . . . . . . . . . . . . . . . . . . . . . . . . . . . . . . . . . . . . . . . . .

There are many ways to ensure standard configuration on an endpoint. For example, Group Policy is one useful tool. Unfortunately, it is highly unlikely any one system will cover all your configuration requirements. However, whatever methods you choose, there is always a way to change settings if the user has an administrative account.

A big advantage of standard user accounts is the fact that they aid change and configuration management. When an administrator logs onto a machine, there is the potential that the system's configuration may undergo unsanctioned changes. A Privilege Management solution helps to maintain the intended configuration of a system, but at the same time gives the flexibility to change sanctioned items.

Least privilege security enables system administrators to maintain better-standardised environments and reduce support costs. If the service desk can be certain of a system's configuration, it is much easier to support that system. If users can make changes to important configuration settings, IT support staff are faced with a much more difficult job, which increases the resolution time.

Least privilege security also prevents users from circumventing controls implemented by system administrators. If a user has an administrative account, with enough knowledge, it is possible to circumvent any security solution. Ultimately, if a user has an administrative account, there is likely a way to break into a system even if other controls are in force.

Good change and configuration management provides stability. Computers do not stop working without reason; normally something or someone made a change.

## 5.4. Application control is easy (trust me!)

Removing administrator accounts should not be viewed as a panacea for all security-related problems. It is still possible that malware could install itself by exploiting an unpatched security vulnerability, which might have otherwise required administrative privileges to install. In addition, there are thousands of applications that are designed in a portable or a per-user form. These can be installed without an administrative account.

As a result, least privilege security alone cannot prevent all unauthorised software appearing on your network and should be used in conjunction with an Application Control (AC) solution. Malware could still infect a fully patched system running with least privilege, although the damage will be limited to the user's profile (in most cases). This damage limitation mechanism, provided by least privilege security, makes any malware outbreak on your network less serious and easier to clean up.

**Privilege Management makes whitelisting easy:** if all users are given standard user privileges; they are locked down and cannot change the build - as such you can trust and whitelist large areas of it.

This allows rules which trust the operating system, line of business applications and prohibits unauthorised applications to be applied. In short, only allow what is trusted to run. I have included an overview below; chapter 7 provides greater implementation detail:

**Trusted Locations:**

- **Windows System (%systemroot%):** The operating system can be defined by the location and items signed within the WindowsSecurity Catalog and therefore it is easy to identify and trust. Should OS functions trigger administrative privileges, they can be seamlessly elevated, or the user prompted to enter an authorisation code by the Privilege Management solution.

- **Line of business applications (%programfiles%):** In most cases, the trusted line of business applications will be installed in program files (other locations can also be defined) by either a deployment technology or a real system administrator. In either case, the rules can be tweaked to allow an application in this location to run if it matches trusted criteria such as if an application has been digitally signed, installed by SCCM or a trusted administrator (trusted owner). Further rules can be applied to identify if it requires elevation and, if so, seamlessly elevate or prompt the user.

Tip: Look for a solution that can deal with complex parent and child scenarios. For example, should a trusted line of business application create and access files within the user temp directory, the solution must be able to establish if the parent process is trusted.

 Within macOS the majority of applications are located in /Applications and the OS is located in /System. Note the forward slash, not backwards as in Windows.

- **Deployment locations & Support tooling:** Consideration should be given to software distribution locations on network drives and locally on the endpoint. Support tooling deployed to areas of the build will also need whitelisting. Again this is made easier by solutions that provide default configurations which include common tools.

### Untrusted locations

- User's profile (%userprofile%): There should be no reason why a line of business application would need to run from the user's profile. The profile is one of a few locations where the user has write access once administrative privileges have been removed. Therefore, malware and malicious users will try to exploit this location. Prohibiting the execution of code from here will thwart the vast majority of attacks.

**Within the macOS the user has a "home" where they can write and run programs from /Users.**

- There are areas like the "temp" folder, SCCM cache and print spooler that standard users can write two; these should be controlled. There are two ways to do this; 1) blacklist these locations, and 2) whitelist only the trusted areas. The second approach is widely viewed as more scalable. Check these locations are current before implementing as they are subject to change.

With this pragmatic approach to whitelisting (location-based), there is no need to create long lists of allowed applications, thus significantly reducing the deployment lifecycle.

 **If you analyse all the attacks over the last 12 months, most of them have tried to utilise administrative accounts and drop a payload to disk. If the malware cannot utilise administrative account or drop a payload to disk, it is severely curtailed!**

## Better together

We have already explored how Privilege Management makes Application Control easy. However, it is not just about the ability to trust locations. In today's modern world end-users require a fluid and dynamic experience, so an application may not only need to run, but may require, elevated privileges. It may need to update an application or configure an operating system function. Elevation of privileges and application execution cannot be viewed as two isolated use cases.

By combining PM and AC, a flexible execution experience is achieved. Good applications are allowed to run, and genuine elevation requests are serviced appropriately. Exceptions that fall outside of these rules can be handled by providing multiple break the glass options, without compromising user experience or security. Look for a solution that combines Privilege Management and Application Control with the same reusable rule set.

## Attack vectors mitigated by Application Control

Here are some worked examples of the types of attacks Application Control can prevent:

* Block executable payloads and scripts dropped to disk by exploited applications (Java, Flash, Adobe Reader etc.)
* Fake updates and files (Flashupdater2k.exe or springbreakpics.pdf. exe) from pop-ups, email attachments and browsing
* APTs and exploit kits, as these are almost always modular and drop files to disk
* Infected content on external media (USB, HDD, DVD etc.) containing malware executables
* Prevents payload stage of an attack (Stage 1 exploit the vulnerability to gain Remote Code Execution, Stage 2 drop and execute payload)
* Drive-by downloads (malvertising, targeted attack, watering hole ww0etc.)
* Social engineering of the user ("run this for me", "install this" etc.)
* Prevents unwanted applications being installed and introducing vulnerabilities (uTorrent etc.)

## 5.5. Detection is dead – sort of

At a time when the IT environment is more diverse than ever, it is not enough to simply sit back and trust in reactive technologies, such as anti-malware, or detection based solutions. Anti-malware solutions simply cannot keep up with the volume of threats. Between 70 and 90 per cent of malware is unique to your organisation - meaning it is highly targeted and therefore unknown to anti-malware vendors[29].

Anti-malware technologies are fighting a losing battle against an increasingly sophisticated malware threat landscape. Attackers often penetrate user endpoints with new malware that eludes the detection tools. Examples of such attacks include bootkit viruses that execute before the OS boots and fileless malware, which hides in the Microsoft Windows registry and deletes all traces of itself from the file system. These are increasing every day.

While 92 per cent of organisations have up-to-date anti-malware software in use today, only 34 per cent rate it as effective in preventing cyber intrusions, according to Ponemon's 'Cyber Strategies for Endpoint Defence' report. When I refer to anti-malware, I am generally referring to all detection technologies, such as antivirus, Host and network-based IPS. In its '5 Reasons Why Your Antivirus Software is not Enough' report, Trend Micro claimed that the software often struggles against sophisticated threats, which keep malware routines out of plain sight.

What's more, anti-malware is looking for known bad files and behaviour, which APTs can bypass to move within a network without detection. IDG Connect explained that malware makers had found a way to circumnavigate detection by "morphing" their code. Morphing changes the code so that viruses look different to anti-malware tools.

29    2015 Data Breach Investigations Report, Verizon, April 2015

In the modern cybersecurity environment, anti-malware also does not offer protection against internal threats. Admin users can disable and override anti-malware settings, leaving systems vulnerable to internal attacks and breaches.

## The Eggshell theory – The latest incarnation of detection

As I mentioned at the start of the book, I have seen many organisations invest in perimeter technology to contain or block threats before they hit the endpoint. This technology, such as network-based detection and sandboxing, has a part to play, but if you do not secure the endpoints first, you end up with an eggshell security stance, where you are reliant on a single outer shell to protect your data. Without secure endpoints, even one small crack in your defences will leave you exposed. Additionally, the world is rapidly changing; employees are often disconnected from the network and work anywhere. This means the only asset you can control and secure is the endpoint.

When you look at some of the big US data breaches, a number had implemented the latest and greatest "next gen" network security technologies, which had "detected" the threats and raised warnings. The problem was that there was so much noise generated by the solutions that no one prevented the attacks happening, as thousands of other false alerts flooded in daily. This is part of the battle when you are looking to detect threats, especially at a network level. It can be like looking for a needle in a haystack.

Network defences face an almost impossible trade-off between security and usability. You want threats to be deeply analysed, but you cannot make the user wait. This results in rash decisions being made by the solution, or network security features being disabled. Intel Security found that over 30 per cent of organisations disable network-based security features to boost speed. Malware authors know this and therefore will create attacks that simply lie dormant for a period to bypass the network sandbox.

**Malware has rapidly evolved to evade network sandboxes using a variety of techniques, including:**

- Delayed onset
- Detecting virtualised environment
- Checking the number of CPU cores
- Checking if the user is real (monitor mouse movement etc.)
- Exploiting the virtual environment to escape

If we do not believe the hype and accept that no system is ever 100 per cent secure, we accept that some threats will not be detected - so where will these end up? On the endpoint.

If the endpoint is not robustly secured using proactive DiD, you are reliant on endpoint detection, such as antivirus, to block the threats - essentially the same kind of detection that failed to identify the threat at the network level. In this case, it only takes one threat to breach an organisation; one APT that is not detected and you are breached. In fact, when you look at a lot of network-based solutions, they have accepted this fact and are now looking to detect attacks post-compromise.

Possibly the most worrying aspect of network-based security is that some major network security vendors have been found to be introducing vulnerabilities and backdoors into organisations. Several independent security researchers have detailed flaws that can be exploited by attackers to not only bypass these defences but also gain access to a privileged position on the network.

Let us not forget that the corporate network is not the only way into a system. Mobile users who connect to external networks, USB devices or rogue users can all cause serious damage. How well does a network solution prevent these common attack vectors?

Critical business data is accessed and/or stored on the endpoint. This is where code - either good, bad or unknown – executes and has access to your data.

Network security products are often viewed as a panacea to the latest threats an organisation is battling with. Buy a box, plug it in and wait for a wonderful report that tells you how many threats are blocked. This might seem like a great solution, but in practice, it just serves to give the illusion of a problem solved.

### Reduce the 'Signal to Noise' ratio

Implementing PM and AC enables IT staff to reduce the noise generated by detection solutions; it does this by only allowing sanctioned applications to run and be elevated with admin privileges. Therefore, an activity that is detected will more likely be rogue than a false positive.

Detection still has a part to play, but it only becomes valuable and relevant once your IT staff can exert control over your enterprise network (PM and AC facilitate this). Its potency is reducing, and if you rely too heavily on it, it may leave you exposed.

## 5.6. Patch, patch! Oh – and patch!

Patching is another very important part of DiD, and it is still the best way to plug known code vulnerabilities. In its 'Labs Threat Report', McAfee named patches as one of the best defences against macro malware attacks. By applying patches quickly and keeping them up to date, you close the door for malware and hackers to exploit flaws in your adopted software. Technology exists to proactively scan for vulnerabilities and address known flaws to reduce the risk of systems being compromised.

According to research from CIO, 50 per cent of chief information officers considered out of date security patches to be the number one threat to their security[30]. However, many organisations overlook the need to handle time dependant exceptions. Understanding and managing vulnerabilities require significant time, attention, and resources. Some automated patching tools may not detect or install certain patches. On their own, they are unable to track, trace and destroy attacks.

When administrative accounts have been removed, users will no longer be able to apply ad hoc, user-initiated, patches. This highlights the need for a privilege management solution that can enable the elevation of update packages for applications without the need for an administrative account.

## Perfection is not possible, but get as close as you can

It is not always practical or quick for a large organisation to keep all of its endpoints fully patched, due to compatibility and geographical diversity. With this in mind, it is crucial a patch management solution is in place.

Nothing is perfect, but the solutions outlined in chapter 4 will improve the situation, so choose the one that is the closest to your needs.

If we cannot be 100 per cent patched 100 per cent of the time, this poses the question; 'how do we protect trusted applications when patches do not exist or cannot be applied?'

---

30    http://www.cio.com/article/2896715/security0/1-cyber-security-threat-to-information-systems-today.html

## 5.7. **Protect the Trusted!**

Once the above technologies are in place, you will have significantly reduced the attack vector on your endpoints. Now you need to turn your attention to exploits which can occur in trusted applications. Zero-day exploits and fileless malware in the known good (trusted) apps will exist, as well as trusted applications being tricked into performing malicious activity. Malware attack chains commonly seek to drop and launch an executable or abuse a native Windows application such as PowerShell. We need to protect against these unknown threats and zero-day attacks that might exploit a vulnerability or leverage before it is closed by a patch. A good way to do this is to apply context-aware application control.

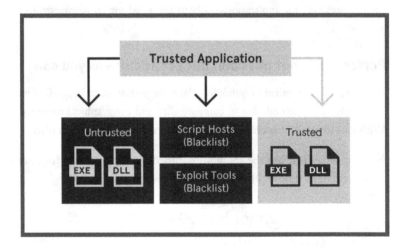

### Context-aware application control

If we look at Internet Explorer, for instance, there should be no need for it to execute a "command and control" child process or run applications which are not part of its installation binaries (normal behaviour).

Therefore, it is straightforward to create tight controls for productivity applications, such as:

- Word
- Excel
- PowerPoint
- Outlook
- Adobe
- Browsers

Another typical scenario is an end-user being socially engineered to click a link or open a Word document that proceeds to download and execute a third party process (not part of the trusted applications installation binaries) that initiates an attack. In this scenarios, Application Control rules can be put in place that prevent Word or Outlook from executing binaries which fall outside its installation set.

It is also common to see malware payloads try to replaced Dynamic Link Libraries (DLLs) of trusted applications with a malicious one. Again, tight "context-aware" Application Control rule can stop this.

## Context is crucially important

Microsoft PowerShell is a tool used by system administrators across the globe. It is extremely powerful and can streamline configuration tasks over across thousands of endpoints. It is also very dangerous in the wrong hands. For example, it can be used to encrypt files and transfer them to offsite locations. I have seen malware which socially engineers a user to open a Word document that proceeds to execute a PowerShell script which encrypts and steals the user's data, as well as data on network shares.

The above, fileless malware example, is extremely difficult for anti-malware technologies to identify. Both Word and Powershell are trusted Microsoft applications, and the action was user-initiated! This is where the power of "context" comes in; there is no genuine business reason for Word to trigger PowerShell. Therefore, by combining Application Control rules which review the parent process (the application that triggered the action), you can quickly prevent this type of attack. The rule would simply block any PowerShell script executed by Word.

**Tip: Look for solutions that provide context-aware application control.**

**Attack vectors mitigated by application control include:**

- Fileless malware
- Unknown processes executed from Trusted Applications
- Script hosts & common exploit tools
- All unknown and untrusted DLLs
- Office Exploits
- Java Exploits
- Flash Exploits
- Browser zero days
- PDF-based attacks, active script and assorted vulnerabilities leading to Remote Code Execution
- Document-based attacks, macros, script and threats such as Sandworm
- Reduces remediation costs for restoring after an attack
- IP theft or ransomware blocked from accessing private data

# 5.8. Endpoint behavioural analysis

Once the above controls have been implemented, you will need visibility over the environment. I am going to focus on the reporting requirements for the PM and AC, given these are the two technologies which can cause the most disruption. Visibility is important for two reasons; 1) establish what has been prevented, and 2) to refine the policies controlling the environment.

You will require detailed auditing and reporting which can provide trend analysis (including explicit application access, application elevation, application execution prevention). Ideally, there should be a feedback loop which allows policies to be refined using this data.

Good reporting should incorporate a rich set of pre-configured dashboards and reports, including executed applications, elevated applications, blocked applications and discovered applications. These should provide detailed summaries of unique applications and processes, including the user and computer where they were executed. These reports help to highlight patterns, behaviours and peak usage.

It is essential that the reports have configurable timeframes - i.e. 24 hours, 7 days, 30 days and 12 months - and advanced filtering options, thus enabling granular customisation.

**You will most likely need the ability to group data by:**

- Application type
- Publisher
- Policy
- Application group
- Users and groups
- Host

The below areas are of specific importance:

## User experience

Understanding user experience will enable you to identify how your users have been interacting with the solution by itemising those who received blocking and elevation messages. If a user sees too many prompts, this will present a poor user experience. Having good visibility will help you tweak your policies to avoid this.

## Application monitoring

Look for a solution that provides insight into:

- **Privileged applications:** Reports on all applications that have been executed with elevated rights, including a breakdown of applications that were elevated automatically and those that were elevated via exception handling.
- **Blocked applications:** Reports on all applications that were blocked as a result of Whitelisting and/or Blacklisting policies.
- **Passive monitoring:** Reports all application usage across protected endpoints to aid software licensing and applicable compliance mandates.

## Discovery

Insight into all applications that require administrative privileges versus those that don't will help with policy design. Trend analysis should be included, which provides items like the Top 10 most used applications and most discovered publishers. Look for a solution that has good integration between reporting and the policy engine to aid policy design.

## Deployment statistics

To aid deployment, the solution should provide detail around its deployment, including the total number of endpoints. Detailed summaries of OS family, device type and language all help with tracking the rollout.

## Policy coverage

To support policy management, the solution must provide policy usage across all managed endpoints, highlighting where policies are taking effect, as well as summarising policies by activity. Coverage reports should show the most and least active policies regarding user and host coverage, as well as application and process enforcements. Policy summaries should provide detailed statistics on individual action relating to users and hosts managed by a policy, and related trend analysis.

## Tamper protection

The solution should provide reporting on any users who have attempted to circumvent the system, by trying to manipulate groups and users. This report must breakdown attempts by the user, computer, the application used and also the individual privileged groups that were protected.

## Context-aware application control

A key insight here will be the number of processes and DLL injections stopped by the solution. It will be important to see the parent-child process hierarchy of the execution chain to establish whether any genuine activity has been blocked - although in my experience this is rarely the case.

## 5.9. Summary - perceptions of defence in depth

The endpoint should be where you start when looking to secure your enterprise against the latest APTs and cyber threats. From here, you can build out. To understand why we do this, remember that a bank does not leave the vault open just because it has a security guard on the door. In business, data and IP is money - so as reassuring as it is to have something watching data coming in and out, if you do not secure the endpoint you risk losing it all.

I have discussed the above approaches with lots of IT professionals who initially expressed concern about the capabilities of a DiD approach. Many worried about layering heterogeneous technologies in an environment, as it often leads to extensive administrative overhead. The perceived labour-intensive nature of DiD has also resulted in concerns about productivity, as its success or failure often depends on those managing and maintaining it. Owners, boards of directors and C-level executives pile on the pressure for IT professionals to protect systems.

I often see IT professionals are made to roll out projects despite them not being ready due to security issues. The need to introduce technology with all of the latest features is frequent, even if there are not the resources in place to manage it. What's more, there seems to be a lack of awareness when it comes to security strategies. For any plan to be successful, there needs to be cooperation, commitment and skill across an organisation. Staff at all levels need to understand the security policies and the part they play in preventing individuals falling prey to schemes such as phishing emails.

According to the Department for Business, Innovation and Skills, in the UK 42 per cent of large organisations do not offer any ongoing security awareness training to staff. 93 per cent of companies claim that where the security policy was poorly understood, staff-related breaches occurred[31].

Part of the problem is that there is not currently enough emphasis placed on the user. Ponemon's 'Cyber Strategies for Endpoint Defense' report found that end users were not high on cybersecurity agendas. Only nine per cent of respondents claim user experience is important when rolling out an information security project, which can create challenges regarding user adoption and satisfaction[32].

Hopefully, you can see the benefits of layering the technologies I have described in this section. However, you may not be convinced it is possible to combine all the technologies without a lot of work and it affects the end user. I would share your concerns if it were not for two reasons; 1) I have done it hundreds of times across millions of endpoints, and 2) the core of your fear will centre around the perceived difficulty of implementing Privilege Management, Application Whitelisting, which is no longer the challenge it once was.

Like anti-virus and patching, which are well understood and can be easily automated, solutions now exist that allow Privilege Management, Application Whitelisting to be managed smoothly.Furthermore, the management of these next-generation tools can be integrated into existing management platforms. This is the key to making this approach smart and simple.

---

31   BIS Information Security Breaches Survey, 2013

32   http://www.ponemon.org/local/upload/file/Cyber%20Strategies%20for%20Endpoint%20 Defense%20Final1.pdf

Let's put the importance of DiD into context. If a piece of malware is not allowed to execute due to the process being unknown and therefore untrusted, there is not much it can do. If it is authorised to run, it will not have any administrative privileges to exploit and will be halted. Consequently, the earlier in the cyber kill chain you can prevent an attack, the more efficient the defence.

A proactive approach allows you to realise this benefit by not waiting until the malware is running or spreading across the network to stop it. Instead, you kill the threat before it starts.

All of this can now be achieved while still allowing users to experience a rich and fluid operating environment. In part three I will discuss the implementation methodology that brings all this together.

**Real world: Security will fail or be circumvented if the user experience is not at the centre of its design. If security gets in the way and users cannot do their job, security will be weakened or turned off completely. I have seen this time and time again at enterprises large and small. Do not underestimate the power of the end user.**

CHAPTER 6

# Defence in Depth and your bottom line

The success of a project can not solely be determined by the technology implementation and little else. To demonstrate value for money, the metrics associated with the financial management aspects of the project must be understood. In addition, it is necessary to align the cost of IT services to business processes to ensure that there is synergy across the business.

A key challenge when it comes to determining ROI (Return On Investment) for security solutions is that many of the benefits are hard to quantify in purely financial terms. This is because much of the damage caused by cyber attacks cannot be easily be communicated via a balance sheet - at least in the short-term.

While immediate costs such as monetary fines, compensation, lost business during downtime and fees charged by external experts to rectify problems are measurable, the hit to a business' reputation, intellectual property and competitive advantage is much more intangible and potentially more significant.

Indeed, according to Ponemon, almost a third of consumer (31 per cent) will stop doing business with a company that suffers a data breach, while 65 per cent will lose trust[33].

Striking a balance between security and freedom brings with it a multitude of benefits, not least of which is a dramatic reduction in TCO (Total Cost of Ownership). This is achieved through the reduced demand on the helpdesk, reduced user downtime and security breach exposure.

While my experience from thousands of deployments across millions of endpoints over nearly a decade shows that implementing DiD security brings with it financial benefits, I do not want you to take my word for it. Fortunately, there is independent evidence from Gartner, Forrester and others that back up my experiences. This chapter aims to guide organisations through building a business case to support the adoption of a best practice Privilege Management and Application Control, within a DiD strategy.

With any business case, it is essential to start with clear business goals. These will differ from organisation to organisation, depending on the starting point and areas of business focus. However, there are some goals that will be common to all businesses, which I'll detail in chapter 7.

It is impossible to provide a one-size-fits-all answer to the ROI you will gain from implementing the technology recommendations discussed in this book. With that in mind, I have focused on the type of calculations you will need to consider when determining your ROI, and have provided some example data for a 2,500 endpoint environment. The benefits identified within this model can broadly be categorised as:

- Reduced demand on the helpdesk
- Reduced end-user downtime

---

33    https://www.centrify.com/about-us/news/press-releases/2017/ponemon-data-breach-brand-impact/

- Reduced security breach exposure
- Improved mitigation

## Information Required

Once the business goals have been outlined and the user requirements defined, it is essential to understand and document the wide-ranging cost and business benefits of implementing a DiD strategy focused on Privilege Management and Application Control approach.

As previously mentioned, there is no "one-size-fits-all" answer to the question of ROI. Here, I describe the items and costs to consider and provide a checklist of the data required to build your calculations. These are categorised into the following areas:

- Costs categories (used in ROI calculations)
- Helpdesk and support data
- Reducing security vulnerabilities data
- Other considerations

Each of these areas will be broken down into key metrics to be collated and critical questions to be explored.

## Cost Categories

**Capital:** This refers to costs that typically apply to the physical assets of your team, department or organisation. They are a factor of production and can be used to produce services, so we may think of capital as encompassing hardware, software and people.

**Operating:** This comprises the day-to-day costs of running the service. Essentially, operating costs ensure the ongoing existence of the solution. The incorporated expenses into this can be monetary, but may also include non-monetary measures such as the time required to accomplish tasks.

**Fixed:** As the name implies, these are costs that do not vary over time unless the price structures are altered. Fixed costs include things like rent or salaries. They also include any rental agreements such as those for hardware or Internet access. The important part about fixed costs is that they are not dependent on the goods or services produced. Therefore, even if your service was only working at 10percent of capacity, the fixed costs would remain the same. These could include items such as server infrastructure to host the technology.

**Variable:** This encompasses costs that vary depending on the volume of goods or services produced or usage. They, therefore, change from month to month, quarter to quarter and year to year. Variable costs depend on usage; therefore if you have any software or hardware that has a usage limitation attached, then there will be increased costs for exceeding the limit. The variable cost includes the total of all marginal costs (the change in total cost when output increases by one unit).

**Direct:** Direct costs are for product and services used only by your solution. For example, included in this category might be your software licences. Another example of a direct cost is if you employed a consultant to work on the project.

**Indirect:** These are the costs that are used by all Service Desk staff, such as heating, lighting and networks. Indirect costs are different from direct costs in that they do not just benefit one particular project - as a result; indirect costs can be difficult to pinpoint and therefore will be left out of my example calculations.

## Helpdesk and Support Data

Giving users the right level of freedom without compromising on security can offer a significant saving on helpdesk and support costs.

Before the ROI can be calculated, the following data will need to be captured:

Note: The below checklists assume support representatives are carrying out these tasks on behalf of the employees.

| Type Of Support Case | Total |
|---|---|

### Environment Information

| | |
|---|---|
| Total number of endpoints in the environment | |
| Percentage Windows | |
| Percentage Mac | |
| Percentage endpoints with LAR (local admin account) assigned to a primary user | |

### Incident Data

| | |
|---|---|
| Number of helpdesk cases logged per month | |
| Number of helpdesk calls that are desktop / laptop related per month | |
| Number of hardware | |
| Number of software | |
| Active X installations | |
| Browser plugin installations | |
| Configuration and installation of printers | |

| | |
|---|---|
| Writing or maintaining custom configuration scripts to work around admin issues | |
| Desktop configuration & maintenance (Disk defrag etc.) | |
| Device connectivity (3G dongles etc.) | |
| Patch management | |
| Desktop power settings | |
| Desktop systems re-imaged (due to user error) | |
| Number of cases due to misconfiguration | |
| Number of helpdesk calls for local admin requests per month | |
| Percentage of helpdesk calls that are follow up calls | |
| Number of helpdesk calls for UAC prompt / requiring elevated privileges | |
| Average resolution time for 1st line calls | |
| Average resolution time for 2nd line calls | |
| Average resolution percentage of helpdesk calls that are follow up calls time for 3rd line calls | |

## Support Costs

| | |
|---|---|
| Annual Salary for a 1st line helpdesk administrator - (£/$/€) | |
| Annual salary for a 2nd line helpdesk administrator - (£/$/€) | |
| Annual salary of a 3rd line helpdesk administrator- (£/$/€) | |
| Average annual salary for IT Security administrators | |
| Average annual salary for IT Desktop Management administrators | |
| Average annual travel expenditures for 3rd line support visits | |
| Average cost per case (if known) | |

## Security Vulnerabilities

It is often difficult to estimate how much time is spent responding to security alerts and breaches, as this data is often not recorded during a breach and is then forgotten about after the fact. The below table will help you start to quantify the costs for your organisation. Later in the chapter, I use industry averages to help establish a baseline.

| Potential Security Risks | Total Number of Incidents per Year | Average Resolution Time per Incident (total hours) | Average Business Cost per Incident |
|---|---|---|---|
| Unauthorised installations (Google Chrome Portable Applications.) | | | |
| Unlicensed software installation | | | |
| Unauthorised build configuration changes | | | |
| Unauthorised access | | | |
| Theft of information/Data leakage | | | |
| Uninstallation/Overriding of critical controls | | | |
| Encryption of user data | | | |
| Phishing emails resulting in compromise of data | | | |
| Malware / Virus / Worm / Trojan attacks | | | |
| Corruption of user systems | | | |
| Financial fraud | | | |

## Other Considerations

The above is designed to measure the tangible cost saving to the business of avoiding these incidents. There are many factors which impact the wider business and bring additional benefits, such as:

- Brand
- Reputation
- Share price
- Fines and litigation costs

I've included a number of areas which often prove hard to quantify.

### Unmanaged Devices

In many organisations, devices where administrator accounts are granted to a user fall outside of company security policies and are therefore defined as unmanaged, with no access to the corporate environment.

In these cases, there is still an inherent risk to the organisation from these devices and users running with administrator accounts. There are several key questions administrators must ask regarding these devices.

- Are users accessing corporate cloud-based services?
- Are users working on corporate data on unmanaged devices?
- Are users using unlicensed or illegal software for corporate purposes?

Whilst, given the unmanaged nature of these devices, it is difficult to quantify the risk, it is still there and must be included in any business case designed to address it.

## Service Level Agreements and User Productivity

When reviewing the above information, it is also important to consider the relationship between the service desk and the user and how one can impact the other.

Does your service desk offer a service level agreement (SLA) and if so, what is it and what impact could this have on user productivity? For example:

- If a request for a software install is classified as low priority and the SLA is five days for this classification, what is the business impact of this delay?
- Will the user be unable to complete their task without service desk assistance?
- What is the cost of lost productivity?

There is also the impact on the service desk. If there is high demand for services because the user experience is too rigid, what percentage of calls logged miss the SLA?

- Is there a penalty for nonconformance to SLAs?
- What is the cost in both financial and perception terms?

## Vulnerability Response and Mitigation

It is essential to measure your organisation's ability to prevent critically vulnerable applications from executing in the environment as quickly as possible, as well as determine your ability to mitigate the vulnerability in the first place. This is a risk calculation, and considerations should include:

- What is the typical time to patch on notification of a critical vulnerability?

- How many times does this happen outside of the typical patching process?
- What is the window of risk where exploits can be executed?

### Application Packaging and Distribution

Within any user environment, there are some application packaging, patching and distribution considerations:

Individual user application requirements – are these currently serviced by the helpdesk or by the packaging teams? What is the cost of packaging and patching applications for a single user?

Limited demand 'line of business' applications – as above, is the packaging team providing a full packing and subsequent patching service for small groups of users, such as developers, marketing teams or data scientists? What is the cost and time attributed to this?

How are self-updating applications from trusted publishers, such as Google Chrome and Adobe Reader, currently being patched by the packaging teams when standard users cannot complete the action? If users could perform these actions themselves without the need for further interaction, what would the cost and business benefit be?

### User satisfaction

Feedback from HR has cited technology as having an adverse effect on user performance and satisfaction in their role. Users are aware of the capabilities and flexibility of modern technology from their consumer experience and expectations are rising that the same user experience should be available at work. Further evidence suggests this is having a knock on, negative impact on attracting and retaining talent and the 'employer brand'.

Again, whilst an organisation may not have access to specific, quantifiable data to support this, it is a factor that must be included in the business case for a modern, flexible workplace.

Implementing a solution that allows an organisation to provide the right level of productivity, flexibility, self-service and security to users has other wide-ranging benefits. Some can be calculated in direct ROI (as above), while other benefits are not necessarily as easy to quantify but must be considered in any supporting business case.

### Governance and Compliance

Finally, under governance and compliance, both security and legal obligations must be considered. The business case must allow for any compliance mandates your organisation are bound by (e.g. PCI DSS, HIPAA, DFARS, NIST).

- Do any of the mandates include the control of administrators and applications running in the corporate environment?
- If so, what are the implications (including fines) of non-compliance?
- Are there procedures in place to prevent data leakage via non-compliant software installs - e.g. Dropbox - or consuming unlicensed content through streaming applications such as uTorrent?

Finally, can your organisation realise benefits from genuinely understanding what software is not only installed but is actually in use in your environment?

- For example, there could be 5000 installs of Visio across the estate, but in the last 12 months, only 500 users have run the application – could this offer a license cost saving?
- Could the control and audit of this usage assist in managing application licensing in a thin client environment?

## Calculating the tangible

ROI is the value of money gained or lost on an investment relative to the amount of money invested. ROI is used to justify the investments that businesses make and is an incredibly useful tool for providing tangible evidence of the value of a solution or service (investment). ROI can also be used before the investment to understand what kind of financial return will be realised – this is often referred to as a cost/benefit analysis.

**One simple formula for calculating ROI is:**

> Gain from investment – Cost of investment / Cost x 100

A good starting point for anything related to ROI is to perform a cost/benefit analysis. This would involve looking at the loss of productivity and revenue if your solution did not exist. It is necessary is to understand users' profitability per hour and then work out how much downtime would be experienced if you were breached or a user could not perform an action. To do this, you will need to understand the salaries of the organisation's staff and their productivity value. The above checklists will help gather the information needed to calculate these figures.

ROI compares investment returns and costs by constructing a ratio or percentage. In most ROI methods, an ROI percentage greater than 0% means the investment returns more than its cost. When potential investments compete for funds (where all other factors genuinely equal), the business-case with the higher ROI is considered, the better choice.

One problem with ROI is that it says nothing about the likelihood that expected returns and costs will appear as forecast. ROI by itself cannot calculate the risk of an investment- it shows merely how returns compare to costs if the action or investment brings the results hoped for.

For that reason, a good business case or an excellent investment analysis will also measure the probabilities of different ROI outcomes, and wise decision makers will consider both the ROI magnitude and the risks that go with it. Decision makers will also expect practical suggestions from the ROI analyst on ways to improve ROI by reducing costs, increasing gains or accelerating gains.

### Example: Simple ROI for Cash Flow and Investment Analysis

What is the ROI for a new system that is expected to cost £550,000 over the next five years and deliver an additional £650,000 in increased profits during the same time? With simple ROI, incremental gains from the investment are divided by investment costs.

- (Gains less Investment Costs) divided by (Investment Costs) * 100
- (£650,000 less £550,000) divided by (£550,000) * 100 = 18%

## Building an ROI Calculator

The assumptions below are designed help you develop an ROI calculator and thus evaluate the financial impact of removing administrator accounts and implementing PM & AC solution. The values used are from independent third-party sources, customer examples and expert opinion. The calculation examples are grouped by Admin-User, Standard-User and Security Breach; these savings are then aggregated.

**Note: The results provided in this example are from an organisation of 2,500 endpoints which are moving from a mixed administrator and standard user environment to a fully managed standard user environment.**

## Operating cost data

It is not always easy to collect the operating costs for every aspect of your environment. Therefore I'm using data collected by Gartner in its "Desktop Total Cost of Ownership report-G00246705". The report includes cost data from the following four scenarios:

- **Unmanaged:** Users have administrator accounts, can install applications and change settings; little to no management tools are being used.

- **Somewhat managed:** Users have administrator accounts, some management tools are implemented, but processes and policies are not fully developed.

- **Moderately managed:** Users have administrator accounts, tools and good processes and policies are in place; users can install some software (blacklisting is in place) and change some settings.

- **Locked and well-managed:** Users are standard users, there are tools, processes and policies; users cannot install software (whitelisting is in place) or change critical settings.

The report finds that moving from a moderately managed environment to a locked and well-managed environment can save 44 per cent in operating costs. The majority of the savings come from reduced user downtime and IT staff having to fix problems caused by users having the ability to misconfigure their machines. The data in this report is for a typical 2,500 endpoint environment.

| | Unmanaged | Somewhat Managed | Moderately Managed | Locked and Well Managed |
|---|---|---|---|---|
| Hardware | $214 | $213 | $212 | $209 |
| Hardware Maintenance | $32 | $32 | $33 | $34 |
| Software | $632 | $606 | $579 | $526 |
| Software Maintenance | $126 | $121 | $116 | $105 |
| IT Software | $70 | $75 | $79 | $88 |
| Data Center Allocation | - | - | - | $0 |
| Electricity/heating/cooling | $67 | $54 | $47 | $23 |
| Hardware, Software, and Facilities | $1,141 | $1,101 | $1,066 | $986 |
| Tier 1 | $147 | $121 | $115 | $102 |
| Tier 2 | $158 | $135 | $111 | $63 |
| Tier 3 | $71 | $70 | $64 | $52 |
| Security | $68 | $62 | $56 | $44 |
| Desktop Management | $105 | $164 | $156 | $139 |
| IT Operations | $549 | $552 | $502 | $401 |
| Administration | $50 | $48 | $46 | $42 |
| Management | $40 | $40 | $40 | $40 |
| User Training | $12 | $13 | $14 | $15 |
| IT Training | $13 | $14 | $14 | $14 |
| Disposal | $30 | $30 | $30 | $30 |
| Administration | $145 | $145 | $143 | $140 |
| Training | $467 | $458 | $448 | $429 |
| Fixing | $924 | $777 | $630 | $336 |
| Downtime | $171 | $136 | $101 | $30 |
| End User Costs | $1,562 | $1,371 | $1,179 | $796 |
| Hardware and Software | $1,141 | $1,101 | $1,066 | $986 |
| IT Operations Labor | $549 | $552 | $502 | $401 |
| Administration Labor | $145 | $145 | $143 | $140 |
| Direct Costs | $1,835 | $1,798 | $1,711 | $1,526 |
| End User Costs | $1,562 | $1,371 | $1,179 | $796 |
| TCO | $3,397 | $3,169 | $2,890 | $2,322 |

## Admin-User Calculations

This section covers the savings gained from removing administrator accounts. Your calculations should include costs and benefits which detail the savings made from IT and end-user productivity improvements, as well as the investment made in the installation of a solution. I have included a number of example calculations below.

**ROI** should calculate the efficiency of your investment and is calculated as follows:

$$\text{ROI} = \text{Total Savings-Total Cost/Total Costs}$$

**Net savings** can be used to show the difference between the total savings over the life of the project less the total cost to purchase the solution:

$$\text{Net Savings} = \text{Total Savings} - \text{Total Costs}$$

**Efficiency saving** shows both the annual IT cost savings and the End User cost reductions over the life of the project. This is calculated by:

1.  Finding the IT cost per user (IT Costs X Number of IT employees)/ Number of End Users)

2.  IT Operations Savings = IT Cost per user X Number of End Users X term of the project (years)

3.  End User Savings = End User Cost per desktop X Number of End Users X term of the project (years)

Note: Review the Gartner data for a good starting point, then refine the data to your operating environment.

The graph below provides an example ROI for a 2,500 endpoint environment, which has removed admin accounts over 36 months. These figures have been established by calculating costs of owning the solution and the savings based on Gartner's findings. I have used very conservative figures in the calculations and assumed the full benefits of the solution would not be gained until month six. With that in mind the ROI is still very good, but remember these calculations only take into account the removal of admin accounts.

## Costs of owning the solution

| Potential Security Risks | QTY | Value | 36 months |
|---|---|---|---|
| Cost per license | 2500 | £20.00 | £50,000.00 |
| Support for 36 months | 2500 | £11.00 | £27,500.00 |
| IT admin cost per year | 0.1 | £5,782.80 (cost estimated from Gartner data) | £17,348.39 |
| Consultancy Days | 8 | £995.00 | £7,960.00 |
| Training Days | 0 | £1,250.00 | |
| Internal set up costs and time | 1 | £6,000.00 | £6,000.00 |
| Total Costs over 36 months | | | £108,808.39 |

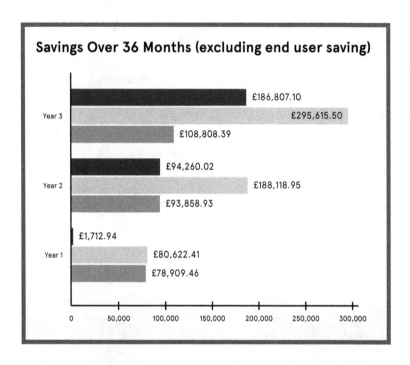

Savings Over 36 Months (excluding end user saving)

| Year | TCO | Efficiency Saving | Net Saving |
|---|---|---|---|
| Year 1 | £78,909.46 | £80,622.41 | £1,712.94 |
| Year 2 | £93,858.93 | £188,118.95 | £94,260.02 |
| Year 3 | £108,808.39 | £295,615.50 | £186,807.10 |
| Total 3 Year Savings | | | £282,780.07 |

## Calculating the ROI

1. £282,780.07 − £108,808.39 = £173,971.68
2. £173,971.68 / £108,808.39 *100 = **160% ROI**

## Standard User (Self-Service) Calculations

The previous section focused on the savings that can be made from removing admin accounts. In these calculations, we will look at the gains made by empowering users to self-service their needs. I have included averages and typical quantities for a 2,500 endpoint environment in the example below.

**Average cost per incident:** Number of hours spent dealing with each IT support issues X Average IT personnel hourly wage rate).

**Mitigation percentage:** Represents the percentage by which the installation of a solution will reduce these costs.

**Average end-user cost per hour:** I am assuming that the end-user costs are the same as the costs of time spent by IT (1-to-1 ratio). In reality, this is more likely to be a 2-to-1 ratio (double end-user costs).

## Standard user (self-service) calculations table

| Support Call Types | Daily | Mitigation Potential | Yearly | Cost per Incident | Cost per Day | Cost per Year | Mitigation Saving | End User Productivity Cost per Day | End User Productivity Cost per Year | Mitigated end user productivity savings per Year |
|---|---|---|---|---|---|---|---|---|---|---|
| Hardware OS | 15 | 85% | 3,795 | £5.38 | £80.70 | £20,417.10 | £17,354.54 | £80.70 | £20,417.10 | £17,354.54 |
| Software install | 15 | 80% | 3,795 | £5.38 | £80.70 | £20,417.10 | £16,333.68 | £80.70 | £20,417.10 | £16,333.68 |
| OS Changes | 12.3 | 70% | 3,120 | £5.38 | £66.35 | £16,787.39 | £11,751.18 | £66.35 | £16,787.39 | £11,751.18 |
| Printers | 3.3 | 85% | 843 | £5.38 | £17.93 | £4,537.13 | £3,856.56 | £17.93 | £4,537.13 | £3,856.56 |
| Engineer attend site | 0.8 | 100% | 202 | £30.00 | £24.00 | £6,072.00 | £6,072.00 | £24.00 | £6,072.00 | £6,072.00 |
| Win7 Migration Support issues | 0 | 100% | 0 | £40.00 | – | – | – | – | – | – |
| Messaging that means support call is avoided... whats happened and why – customer experience | 0 | 100% | 0 | £7.50 | | | – | – | – | – |
| OS Functionality | 0 | 100% | 0 | £18.00 | – | – | – | – | – | – |
| Managing an ad hoc admins group | 0.4 | 100% | 101 | £20.00 | £8.00 | £2,024.00 | £2,024.00 | £8.00 | £2,024.00 | £2,024.00 |
| Automating into support | 0 | 100% | 0 | £1.00 | – | – | – | – | – | – |
| Packaged Apps | 0.4 | 100% | 101 | £250.00 | £100.00 | £25,300.00 | £25,300.00 | £100.00 | £25,300.00 | £25,300.00 |
| Win7 UAC | 0 | 75% | 0 | £18.00 | – | – | – | – | – | |
| Blocking Portable Application (e.g. dropbox) | 0 | 25% | 0 | £18.00 | – | – | – | – | – | |
| TOTAL | 47.3 | $145 | 11,958 | $140 | | £95,554.73 | £82,691.95 | | £95,554.73 | £82,691.95 |

**Mitigated support savings (direct costs) over 36 months:** Mitigation saving x 3

**Mitigated end-user productivity savings over 36 months:** Mitigated end-user productivity saving per year x 3

In the above example, the total three-year saving is **£496,151.72,** based on a 1-to-1 ratio of end-user costs and IT costs. This is very low but still produces a healthy saving. Your savings are likely to be a lot higher.

If we combine these savings with the admin account example with have the following ROI

1.  £282,780.07 + £496,151.72 = £778,931.79
2.  £778,931.79 – £108,808.39 = £670,123.4
3.  £670,123.4 / £108,808.39 *100 = **615% ROI**

Note: The costs of owning the solution were included in the previous example.

## Breach Mitigation ROI Calculations and Assumptions

So far, we have looked at data and calculations focused on the ROI gain from user productivity and IT management. An essential but often difficult to quantify ROI benefit is security breach mitigation. Due to the difficulty in calculating these figures I have used industry averages. It is essential to review these averages and ensure they apply to your organisation. Below are five areas to consider:

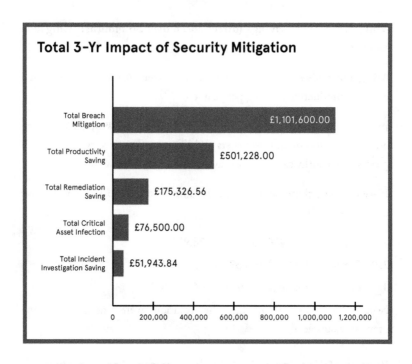

## Reduce Risk of a Security Breach

The calculations used here are taken from data gathered by industry bodies such as Ponemon, McAfee and Gartner.

**A.** Expected cost of a major security breach = £3,600,000*

**B.** Probability of a breach = 0.24**

**C.** The average annual cost of data breaches = £432,000 (A*B/2)

**D.** Reduced risk with DiD = 85% (see below)

**E.** Annual Benefit Year 1 = £367,200 (C*D)

**F.** Annual Benefit Year 2 = £367,200 (C*D)

**A.** Annual Benefit Year 3 = £367,200 (C*D)

**Total Breach Mitigation £1,101,600.00**

*Ponemon Cost of Data Breach Study
**Probability of a breach in the next 2 years:

- Arabian Cluster - 0.31
- Australia - 0.16
- Brazil - 0.4
- Canada - 0.17
- France - 0.32
- Germany - 0.15
- India - 0.31
- Italy - 0.22
- Japan - 0.24
- South Africa - 0.33
- United Kingdom - 0.23
- United States - 0.24

2016 Cost of Data Breach Study: Global Analysis. Ponemon Institute

## Reduction in infection

Defence in depth has many well-documented benefits; the Australian Signal directive estimates there is an 85 per cent reduction in the infection rate by implementing the technologies discussed in this book.

### Reduce downtime due to critical asset infection

This value driver focuses on the value of reducing server outages as a result of an infection that could have otherwise been prevented.

A. Current total number of critical assets = 500 (Total production servers)

B. Percent of critical assets requiring remediation annually = 0.1%

C. Total number of critical asset remediations annually = 0.5 (A*B)

D. The average downtime per critical asset during remediation = 2.0 Hours

E. The estimated cost of critical asset downtime per hour = £30,000 per Hour = (See below)

F. Reduction in server infection and remediation time due to DiD = 85% (See below)

G. Annual benefit Year 1 = £25,500 (C*D*E*F)

H. Annual benefit Year 2 = £25,500 (C*D*E*F)

I. Annual benefit Year 2 = £25,500 (C*D*E*F)

**Total Critical Asset Infection £76,500.00**

## Cost of critical asset downtime

- Ponemon Institute (December 2013) – $474k/hr
- IDC (Nov-Dec 2014) – $100k/hr or $500k+/hr for critical failure
- Veeam (Dec 2014) – $105k/hr or $130k/hr for critical failure
- Infonetics (Feb 2015) – up to $100MM/yr
- Gartner - $42,000 per hour

## Reduction in infection

Defence in depth has many well-documented benefits; the Australian Signal directive estimates there is an 85 per cent reduction in the infection rate by implementing the technologies discussed in this book.

### Reduce productivity impact of endpoint infection rates for IT and End-Users

A. The average number of endpoints infected annually = 1,008

B. Productivity impact per infection IT = £130

**C.** Productivity impact per infection End-User = £65

**D.** The total annual cost IT = £131,040 (A*B)

**E.** The total annual cost End-User = £65,520 = (A*C)

**F.** Reduction due to DiD = 85%

**G.** Annual benefit Year 1 = £167,076 ((D+E)*F))

**H.** Annual benefit Year 2 = £167,076 ((D+E)*F))

**I.** Annual benefit Year 3 = £167,076 ((D+E)*F))

**Total Productivity saving £501,228.00**


**Reduced Time Spent on Remediation Planning**

**A.** Current number of admins that perform remediation planning = 5

**B.** Percent of their time dedicated to remediation planning = 25%

**C.** Total FTEs dedicated to remediation planning = 1.3 FTEs (A*B)

**D.** Reduction in effort due DiD = 75%

**E.** FTEs saved due to DiD = 0.94 FTEs (C*D)

**F.** Average annual salary = £56,000

**G.** Average annual growth in remediation planning = 10%

**H.** Annual benefit Year 1 = £52,968 (E*F)

**I.** Annual benefit Year 2 = £58,265 ((H*(1+G))

**J.** Annual benefit Year 3 = £64,092 ((I*(1+G))

**Total Remediation saving £175,326.56**

**Reduced time spent querying and investigating security incident alerts and events**

A.  The average number of security incident investigated weekly for endpoints = 50 per Week

B.  The percent of all threats that are investigated that are false positives vs credible threats
    a.  False Positives = 67%
    b.  Credible Threats = 33%

C.  The average IT effort required per incident
    a.  False Positives = 17 Minutes *
    b.  Credible Threats = 17 Minutes*

D.  Reduction to due DiD
    a.  False Positives 85%
    b.  Credible Threats 50%

E.  The total time saved annually
    a.  False Positives = 419 Hours = A*52*B1*C1/60*D1
    b.  Credible Threats = 121 Hours = A*52*B2*C2/60*D2

F.  The average hourly IT admin wage - £32 per Hour

G.  Annual benefit Year 1 = £17,314 (E1+E2)*F

H.  Annual benefit Year 2 = £17,314 (E1+E2)*F

I.  Annual benefit Year 3 = £17,314 (E1+E2)*F

**Total incident investigation saving     £51,943.84**

*Over 705 investigated incidents 198.8 hours were spent investigating them. (16.9 minutes each) – 2015. Ponemon. The Cost of Malware Containment.

## Total Benefits by Benefit Category

The chart and table below break down anticipated benefits across select benefit categories. ABC Company's three-year potential benefits are distributed as follows:

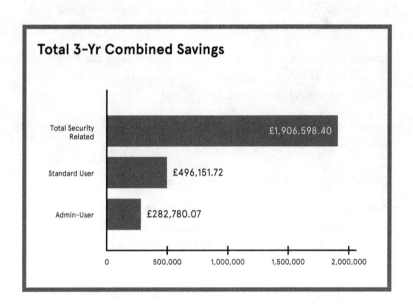

If we combine all the savings we achieve the following ROI

1.  £282,780.07 + £496,151.72 + £1,906,598 = £2,685,529.79
2.  £2,685,529.79 – £108,808.39 = £2,576,721.4
3.  £2,576,721.4 / £108,808.39 *100 = **2368% ROI**

Note: the costs of owning the solution were included in the previous example.

## Summary

As you can see, there are many considerations when building a business case. In this chapter, I have tried to bring together the key indicators you will need to consider when creating your business case. As every environment is different, careful consideration should be given to the calculations and data assumptions to ensure they are fit for purpose.

Even if you significantly scaled back the savings from the ones I have identified above, you should still see a very compelling ROI. In the above example we achieve an ROI of 2,368 per cent.

Please feel free to contact me if you have any questions in regards to the above calculations.

### Map the project to key performance indicators (KPIs)

Mapping security risks to KPIs helps to get acceptance from management for your project. Showing management how it will help better manage security incidents will allow the benefits of the project to resonate.

Nonetheless, looking at a list of KPIs and trying to map them to security issues can be a daunting task. Security incidents affect productivity, compliance and business continuity on a micro level, making it hard to map security risks to high-level KPIs. IT is critical to the operation of every business, so any risk introduced into the computer systems has the potential to affect a large number of a company's KPIs. For example, demonstrating how a security incident and its subsequent downtime will affect a team's ability to hit its target shows that security is a business problem and not just an IT issue.

I appreciate this is not easy and it is often the case that business KPIs simply do not map across. Consequently, I would recommend you create a set of KPIs based on how IT supports the business and its processes. You will need to have a good knowledge of your business to understand the motivations for particular KPIs fully. However, this will not only affect your DiD project, but how IT approaches supporting the business.

**It is like selling insurance against shark attacks!**

Security projects are often hard to sell, and this is especially true when the business has little understanding of security beyond antivirus software and firewalls. Most corporate boards have no-one sitting on them who comes from an IT background, being mainly made up of sales and finance experience. Consequently, they often assume that anti-malware and firewalls are enough.

Security is like selling insurance against shark attacks: No one understands why he or she needs it until it is too late! The problem is, IT security is hard to quantify unless you have a background in computer science. After all, if management cannot see a problem (a shark), they are not worried about insuring against it. Security needs to be presented as a real business problem that affects the company's bottom line. Physical security is easy to see; everyone wants a lock on his or her front door as it is clear what the consequences are. The same should be true of cyber security. What is the risk of not taking proactive action?

Cleaning up the damage after the attack is much harder and more costly than taking steps to reduce the risk of it happening in the first place.

PART THREE

# Implementation Success

CHAPTER 7

# Defence in depth is great in theory – but how do I implement it?

By now, you can hopefully see that prevention is possible. However, if you are like me, your next logical thought will be "how do I implement this?"

During this chapter, I will be bringing to life how DiD is possible. I have developed a two-wave, six phase, nine stage implementation methodology based on my work with thousands of customers. The principles come from PRINCE 2 project management methodology and aim to establish and deliver the following:

- A defined lifecycle
- Defined and measurable business goals
- A corresponding set of activities to achieve the business goals
- A specified amount of resources
- A project structure, with assigned responsibilities, to manage the project

This methodology has proven to be secure and robust in the most demanding of environments. As a result, I have been able to deploy DiD in some of the largest and most diverse organisations. For example, I implemented half a million endpoints with DiD in six months.

 **The methodology is not set in stone and would normally be customised to meet the needs of the organisation – bear this in mind whilst reading.**

## 7.1. The implementation methodology

**Avecto's Deployment Methodology**

Wave-Based Rapid Deployment Approach

| | | Client | | Avecto |
|---|---|---|---|---|
| **Wave 1** | **PHASE 1** Project Design | Wintel / Security / Helpdesk | **1** | Implementation workshop |
| | **PHASE 2** Tech Deploy | Wintel engineering | **2** | Agent & infrastructure deployment |
| | **PHASE 3** Baseline Deployment | Wintel / Security | **3** | QuickStart workstyle customisation |
| | | Comms team | **4** | Internal comms |
| | | Wintel engineering | **\*5** | QuickStart deployment |
| **Wave 2** | **PHASE 4** Layered Workstyles Design | Wintel / Security | **\*6** | Review user behavioural data |
| | | Wintel / Security | **7** | Design layered workstyles |
| | **PHASE 5** Workstyle Deployment | Wintel | **\*8** | Deployment of layered workstyles |
| | **PHASE 6** Project Handover | Helpdesk / Wintel | **9** | BAU support |

**\*** denotes stage may involve multiple iterations
**Wave 1:** significantly improves Security
**Square size:** equates to effort required to complete stage

The methodology has been split into two halves, Wave 1 and Wave 2, within which there are nine stages, as outlined in the above diagram. This allows an organisation to achieve rapid benefits almost overnight. I will first explain the rationale behind this and then provide the detail. The ownership of nine stages is split across the vendor and the customer. The owner of each stage is identified by which side of the centre line it sits on. The size of the circle denotes the effort involved. After each phase I make sure that it is signed off by the customer, thus ensuring they are completely satisfied with the work. You can also see from the bottom section of the diagram the teams that will be required for each phase of the deployment.

## Security balancing act

As previously discussed, every organisation is facing an endpoint security balancing act. On one hand, employees and their endpoints need to be secure. On the other hand, many employees require a free and flexible operating environment. The paradox that exists between these two polarised opposites are what organisations struggle with. Inevitability compromises have to be made, with organisations settling for average security that ultimately results in an unhealthy reliance on detection based technologies, which amount to nothing more than a cat and mouse game.

## A simple and smart approach

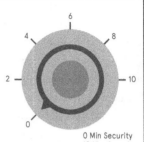

### Rapid Deployment

Increase in Security from Day 1...

### Common Starting Security Posture : 0/10

- All users have full admin rights.
- Users can execute unknown applications.
- Malware can run with elevated privileges.
- Security controls and policies can be bypassed.
- Software installs & execution with no control or visibility.

0 Min Security
10 Max Security

Think of endpoint security on a sliding scale, 0 being least secure and 10 being the security panacea. With this simple and smart approach, you can significantly move up the security scale, quickly and easily, without impeding usability.

**If we take a closer look at the security scale, position 0 would result in the following:**

- Every user has local administrator privileges
- All unknown applications being allowed to run
- All unknown content, emails, downloads etc. being opened with full access to the endpoint
- Ransomware and malicious payloads being able to embed deep into the system

**At the other end of the scale, position 10 would result in:**

- Everyone running with standard user privileges

- Applications requiring elevated privileges will have a custom built privilege token applied, granting only the required privileges.

- Only approved line of business applications being allowed to run and are correctly identified

- Unknown and untrusted applications will be automatically blocked

- Unknown and untrusted content (emails, downloads etc.) will be isolated from the system and the data the user can access.

I see many organisations allowing a significant percentage of their users to log onto their endpoints as local administrators. If you enable this you are effectively at level 0. Corporate policies can be bypassed; security software can be disabled, and users can run and install what they like.

Everybody wants to get their security dial turned all the way up to 10, and with this methodology you can get there. However, it is vital that we make sure the user experience is not hindered during this journey. If our desktops are secured to an extent where the user cannot do their job, there will be resistance, and typically the project will fail.

We need to find the right balance between user freedom and security. The DiD technologies described in chapter 5 will be phased in, and I will recommend the deployment of a baseline workstyle which significantly moves your organisation up the security scale.

## Wave One

### Rapid Deployment

Increase Security from Day 1...

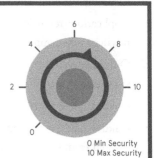

### Avecto Wave 1 'QuickStart': 7/10

- All users run with standard user rights.
- Only applications requiring admin rights can run with elevated privileges.
- Users can execute only known-good applications.
- Unknown and defined unwanted application are blocked.
- Positive experience as users can install new software through customisable messaging with full audit trail.

0 Min Security
10 Max Security

Wave one is focused on enabling the removal of local administrative accounts across your organisation, coupled with a 'three levels' flexibility (Low/Medium/High – more on this later), which automatically detects applications requesting admin privileges and empowers the user to self-elevate for those that don't. The users will be asked for varying levels of secure justification based on an application's risk profile. This allows your end users to continue to work uninterrupted with significantly less risk. If the user introduces unknown/untrusted applications, they can be blocked or asked for secure justification. Similarly, unknown content will run in an isolated and protected area.

This approach will move your organisation to position 6 or 7 of the security scale.

1. All users run with standard user accounts
2. Only applications requiring admin privileges can run with elevated privileges
3. Users can execute only known-good applications
4. Unknown and defined unwanted application are blocked
5. Positive experience as users can install new software through customisable messaging with a full audit trail

A key point to consider here is that administrative accounts have been removed early in the deployment methodology, you have not had to wait for any elongated discovery cycles to complete.

## Wave Two

### Rapid Deployment

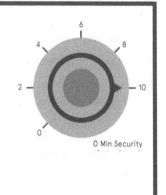

Increase Security from Day 1…

**Avecto Wave 2 Informed Iteration: 10/10**

- Evidence based understanding of user requirements.
- Role based controls and freedoms granted through tailored workstyles.
- Default-deny application whitelisting implemented.
- Orchestration & Integration with workflow tools such as ServiceNow for streamlined exception handling.
- Advanced policy logic to refine except in processing to minimise 3rd party oversight to allow additional flexibility.

For many organisations, 7/10 may be enough, and I have seen many people stop here. Considering they were at 0 before, they are happy. However, for many, that is not enough, and I always advocate striving for 10/10.

Wave two refines the policies deployed in wave one by utilising data gathered from genuine user behaviour. It is crucial the solution you choose gathers accurate user behaviour data, identifying which applications they have run with elevated privileges, which are executing from within the user's profile area and which applications are being installed. This data allows you to build tailored policies that fit your enterprise, elevating only the applications a user requires, enabling only the applications that we trust to run and blocking all unknowns.

More secure layered policies can be gradually rolled out over time, targeting specific roles and needs within your organisation. This moves the security dial closer to 10, while maintaining a positive end-user experience and the ability to handle exceptions with Challenge and Response functionality.

**Wave two: Informed Iteration: 10/10**

1. Evidence-based understanding of user requirements
2. Role-based controls and freedoms granted through tailored workstyles
3. Default-deny application whitelisting implemented
4. Orchestration and integration with workflow tools such as ServiceNow for streamlined exception handling
5. Advanced policy logic to refine exception processing to minimise third party oversight and allow additional flexibility

## 7.2. **Wave one - Stage 1 - Design workshop (start with the end in mind)**

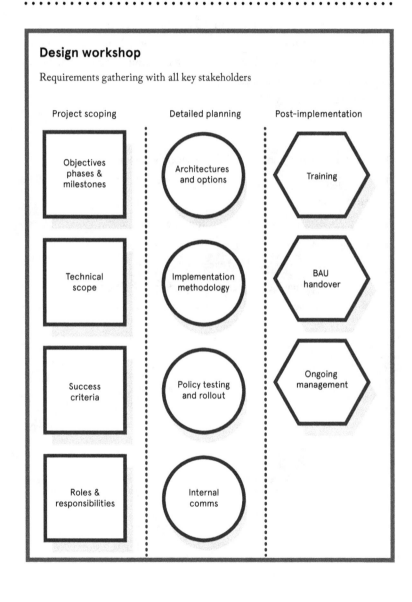

I place a significant emphasis on the design and planning stages of implementation. In order for a detailed Project Initiation Document (PID) to be created, I would hold requirement gathering and design workshops with my clients to launch the project. This should ensure that the key stakeholders from across the business are involved from the outset, which is crucial for a successful adoption. During this consultation period, I work closely with the stakeholders to agree on the key points highlighted in the image above.

 **I have seen projects fail where the technology has been imposed on the business.**

## Defining objectives – what does success look like?

It is important to start with the end in mind! Start with why you are running the project. Once the objectives have been discussed and requirements have been established, you can use these as key measurement criteria (milestones by which your project is measured). I have included a number of questions you can use to establish your requirements and help ascertain the insight you will need.

If you do not understand what success looks like, do not start!

**Typical Business Objectives:**

1.  Follow best practice security controls and significantly reduce risk by eliminating Local Administrator Accounts from the end user environment without impacting user productivity.

2.  Follow best practice security controls and significantly reduce risk by controlling what applications can execute in the end user environment without impacting user productivity.

3.  Achieve compliance and proactively prevent attacks.

4. Improve end user experience – enable users to perform activities that their role requires without interruption and without compromising on security.

5. Provide more flexibility to standard users who have previously been too restricted in line with modern business and technology management.

6. Operational efficiency – ensure that helpdesk tickets are reduced and maintenance is simple.

7. Operate an end user environment where there are no Local Administrators, but where users are empowered to perform the tasks required by their role.

8. Enable a remote, cloud-based 'Modern Management' approach without compromising on security.

### Questions to help establish objectives

1. What is your approach to managing risk based on your need to drive the business' profitability and deliver against the board's objectives/agenda? How free can you afford your users to be?

2. Do you have to meet any compliance mandates such as external and internal quality/compliance/risk systems?

3. Is security seen as an enabler within your business or a box-ticking exercise? Does your business believe you have achieved an ROI out of security in the last three years or is it just seen as mitigating risk?

4. What is the board's view on cybersecurity risks?

5. Do you benchmark your security against your competitors?

6. How do you strike a balance between security of assets and the need for employees to be productive?

7. Have there been outbreaks which have resulted in data or productivity loss?

**Environment questions**

1. What directory services are in use for endpoint management?
   a. E.g. Azure AD, Active Directory, 3rd Party? Are all endpoints under the management scope of this technology?
2. Do you have a delegate security model?
3. Are IT operations centralised or decentralised?
4. Are you using any Mobile Device Management solutions (MDM), i.e. Intune?
5. What Helpdesk / Service desk technologies do you use (eg, ServiceNow)?
6. What is your current approach to User Account Control? Is this on, off or toned down?
7. What are software deployment technologies currently in use, for example, SCCM?
8. Do you maintain a software inventory list and understand the privileges they require?
9. How many diverse groups exist within your environment, such as developers and engineers, for example?
10. Are a number of these remote workers or do they spend a lot of time on the road?
11. What is your approach to end-user experience? Do you have a culture of a free and open environment or is it locked down and controlled?
12. Which Windows operating system(s) is in place?
13. Are you planning a migration to the latest versions of Windows? Desktop and servers?
14. Which legacy Windows operating systems will you need to support? Desktop and servers?

15. Do users have temporary local administrative accounts on the endpoint, depending on the tasks at hand, or permanent privileges?

16. Do you have applications that require local administrator privilege in order to run?

17. Do you have users that need to install peripherals?

18. Do you have users that need to install applications that require the user to be a local administrator?

19. Do you have users that need to run built-in Windows features or functions that require the user to be a local administrator?

20. Do you have a list of applications that you want to deny the user from running?

21. Do you want to create an approved list of applications that users can run

 I spent five days with a large global bank understanding their existing process and procedures and working out its policy landscape. Typically, this would be one to two days.

## Who should be involved?

The project must be well thought out and planned accordingly, as it will touch every endpoint in the environment. DiD solutions require more than just the desktop or server support team be involved, as this is typically not the only team that needs to support the solution and define the goals. Initially, it is important to define the business sponsor(s) and project owner(s). These stakeholders are responsible for ensuring the project receives the funding and attention that it deserves, as well as driving and keeping the project on track.

At the start of the project, all stakeholders will need to be involved. I have provided a list below of the typical teams that would need to participate.

| Stakeholder | Why Required |
| --- | --- |
| Security | The discussions will focus on a defence in depth security strategy. It is therefore important that the requirements of the security team are captured. This will enable the team to design a solution that meets the security standards within your organisation. |
| Infrastructure | Multiple deployment and management platforms will be discussed. Ongoing maintenance will also need to be performed by the appropriate team, and this needs to be considered. The infrastructure teams will need to be consulted to ensure the most appropriate fit for your business. |
| Service Delivery | Whilst the technologies discussed, during the workshop, offer unparalleled security, they also deliver operational savings through end-user empowerment. Therefore it is important to understand the end-user issues related to overlocked or under locked environments. This data can be used to demonstrate operational savings. |
| Human Resources | On occasion, customers will engage with human resources before deploying security tools. There may be considerations around monitoring of users' activity or restricting what the user can or can't do with their computers. If such issues exist within your organisation, we suggest attendance at the workshop by the appropriate representatives. |

## Project management

Defining ownership of the project and lines of communication, both internally and with the vendor, is crucial for success. It is vital that all members of the project team communicate efficiently and work effectively throughout every stage of the project. At a minimum, the following components should be in place during the project and implementation:

- Periodic project update meetings with all team members
- Weekly review of the issues log (this might need to include the vendor support)
- Identify training requirements and ensure training is conducted as soon as possible

## Do I need a desktop refresh to deploy DiD?

In short, the answer is no. Having said that, there are sound technical justifications for installing a new OS at the same time as deploying DiD. A fresh, standardised image with built-in DiD allows us to ensure an issue-free experience and provides additional benefits, such as the extra performance gained from a new install and elimination of undetected software and configuration errors.

If DiD is applied to an existing system, you potentially freeze any existing configuration errors into the system, and you may not see the full benefits.

## The Culture Shock

Understanding the nuances of company culture is crucial to the success of this type of project, or for that matter, any project. I have seen company culture inhibit both innovation and change. People's natural response is to resist change, and this is no less true in the area of computer security, as users almost universally perceive security as an inconvenience which gets in the way of their user experience. However, it does not have to be this way. Security should be an enabler, and hopefully, you have seen through this book that the balance between security and freedom truly can be achieved.

## Understanding Culture

I have implemented DiD security strategies in a whole host of organisations, from those with a few hundred employees to global enterprises with half a million employees. As you can imagine the gulf between these cultures is immense. Obviously, this can affect what can be achieved, and how to go about doing it. Before embarking on a project of this sort you need to understand the culture, as this will drive how the project will be conducted.

**Company culture determines how the employees and management of a company behave. For instance, to what extent do employees:**

- Help one another and contribute to teamwork?
- Co-operate to achieve common goals?
- Respect each other?
- Understand the work of colleagues in other departments?
- Seek to grow?
- Do not reprimand failure, but learn from it and become better?

If the answers to the above are positive, then it is likely that your company has a healthy culture. This will make the project easier to implement, as employees will strive to understand why the project is being run.

If the answer is negative, employees may be defensive, unreasonable, have unrealistic expectations, or be aggressive. IT will find it difficult to get users on side with any new project. However, all is not lost, with the right solution, implementation plan and communication approach, it is still possible to make the project a success. However, it will take a little longer and need more care.

## Build the plan

Following the design workshop, I recommend creating a detailed project scope, Project Initiation Document (PID) and project timeline, clearly highlighting the finer details of the project so that all parties are clear on objectives, requirements and success criteria. We can then establish milestones that will be used to sign off each phase of the project.

The timeline should include the pilot and all stages of the implementation methodology. The project timeline should also include time for project team training, internal communication and end-user training. Additionally, there will need to be time allocated for post-implementation troubleshooting, Business As Usual handover and project closure.

I typically recommend the initial stages of the project timeline should not overlap, but once the team becomes more familiar with the implementation methodology phases, this can change. Each iteration of the project will become quicker and easier as the team becomes more experienced.

 Depending on the size and complexity of your organisation, as well as the complexity of the approval processes, a typical project can be as short as one week or as long as 12 months. I typically see projects averaging between one and three months.

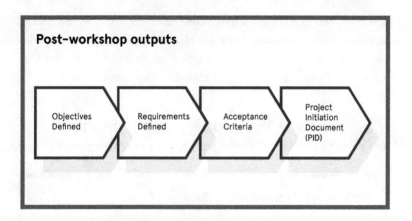

**Post-workshop outputs**

Objectives Defined → Requirements Defined → Acceptance Criteria → Project Initiation Document (PID)

## Buy-in from senior management

Ultimately, success will be defined by user acceptance and support from management. A smooth and trouble-free implementation is in the interest of the business, and in the event that you encounter resistance on the shop floor, it is good to know you have got full backing from management. No one likes being undermined, and I often see projects fail when users push back, and managers simply overrule IT.

Current financial and threat landscapes often play a part; if times are hard, then the lowered TCO will help management get behind the project. If you have just been breached, then the security advantages need to be focused on.

## Aim for 100 per cent

Aim for 100 per cent of your endpoints (desktops and server) to come under the scope of your DiD project. With the right tools and approaches in place (like those outlined in this book), there should be no reason why this is not achievable, in theory. The reality is, the real world is different; there will always be systems and users who are missed, for a myriad of reasons.

The point here is aim high; I have extensive conversations with clients to establish at what percentage they will class the project as complete. With the right tools, you will be able to report on the number of users now running with standard accounts vs administrative accounts and so on.

# 7.3. Stage 2 – Technology deployment

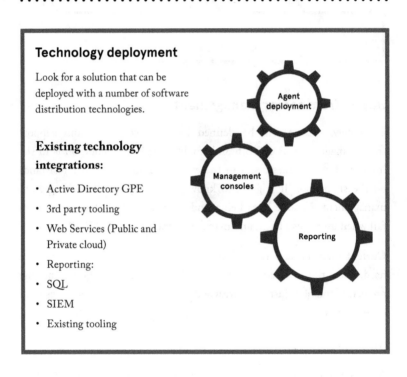

**Technology deployment**

Look for a solution that can be deployed with a number of software distribution technologies.

**Existing technology integrations:**

- Active Directory GPE
- 3rd party tooling
- Web Services (Public and Private cloud)
- Reporting:
- SQL
- SIEM
- Existing tooling

At this point in the project, you will have established your requirements; the next key stage is to make important architecture design decisions.

**There are two approaches in regards to deployment topologies;**

1.  Solutions which leverage existing technologies and integrate tightly
2.  Proprietary deployment systems.

Each method has it owns merits. Therefore it is vital to consider the pros and cons of your environment.

For example, using proprietary systems to deploy policies and agents to the endpoints may add a significant management cost and a high learning curve. On the other hand,a solution that has tight integration with your existing infrastructure could significantly speed up the deployment and reduce cost.

In my experience, a solution that offers hybrid options is fundamental. The larger the organisation, the more likely the need to have endpoints managed by multiple deployment technologies. Make sure these do not run in isolation and can accommodate each other. For example, you may need an endpoint controlled by multiple deployment technologies to deal with situations where the device may connect to the network and work remotely; policy must be applied 100 per cent of the time.

**Areas to consider:**

1.  **Management console integrations** - Does the solution integrate with; Group Policy, Azure AD, Intune, third party platforms, or is it solely standalone?
2.  **Agent deployment** - Can the agent be deployed via SCCM, cloud solutions, does it work remotely, can it integrate into third party platforms?
3.  **Security Model** - Does it have a strong security model that includes delegated administration?
4.  **Policy Management** - Does it support hierarchical policy management for tiered organisational models?

5. **Agent Management** - Can an endpoint be managed by multiple policies to support mixed usages scenarios?

6. **Reporting** - Does the solution provide meaningful reports which can be integrated into existing systems, eg. SIEM, or is all data proprietary?

 When working in large enterprises, I often find that not all of the endpoints fall under the management scope of a single deployment architecture. Therefore, it is important to understand this earlier on in the design stages and plan accordingly. I would also recommend choosing a solution that ensures feature parity across deployment topologies. It is often the case trade-offs need to be made when deciding on architecture.

## Separation of duty

In large enterprises, it is most often the case that the security and operations responsibility is split across multiple teams. Therefore, it is important that your policy can be designed and transferred securely to the teams responsible for deployment. This is achieved by integrating into existing infrastructure, thus utilising the built-in delegation models. In addition, look for solutions that have the ability to digitally sign policy to prevent tampering.

DEFENCE IN DEPTH IS GREAT IN THEORY – BUT HOW DO I IMPLEMENT IT?

225

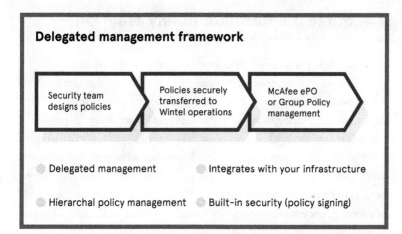

During a deployment of 375K endpoints, IT security ops had the responsibility to create and sanction policy design. However, they had no responsibility to deploy the GPO objects. Therefore I needed provisional IT security with the ability to securely create policy and Wintel operations, as well as the ability to deploy. The crucial requirement here was to ensure Wintel operations could not change policy. This was achieved via policy signing.

# 7.4. **Stage 3 – Baseline policy creation**

It is at this point most organisations, project stakeholders and IT professionals will be reduced to quivering wrecks, as they realise they know next to zero about their end user and application estate. Many organisations I have worked with feel that they need a period of "discovery" to establish which applications, tasks, scripts, installers etc. need administrator privileges and should be allowed to run. This approach was valid in the early days of privilege management and applications control technologies, but not anymore. Hence the two-wave approach I am advocating. For completeness, I will include a section on discovery, but this is rarely used nowadays due to significant technological advances.

## Baseline policy (understanding your use case)

Consulting with business owners and end-user groups will not give you all the answers, and consequently, you need a solution that will allow a policy to be deployed that provides a flexible but controlled user experience on day one. Additionally, it must provide insight into what exact use cases are being utilised, thus allowing further policy refinement.

Most organisations believe a fully automated discovery phase is required to capture the use cases, as this will significantly reduce the deployment time and resource impact. However, in practice this will not work as it typically elongates the deployment lifecycle, the user still has admin privileges, any application can run, and there are often mis-reported requirements due to false positives (raised by badly written applications). With the best will in the world, fully automated discovery will lead to poor policy designs.

As a result, I always recommend a hybrid approach where administrative privileges are removed, and the user is given a flexible admin-like experience. Use cases are captured, analysed and a policy recommendation is provided in wave two of the deployment. It is of the utmost importance that the recommended policy design is ratified by your organisation, tested and then rolled out in tranches (starting small and increasing once testing results are positive).

The approach I recommend uses tried and tested business logic to establish which applications, tasks, scripts, OS functions and installs require administrative privileges and should be allowed to run.

## Baseline Policy design

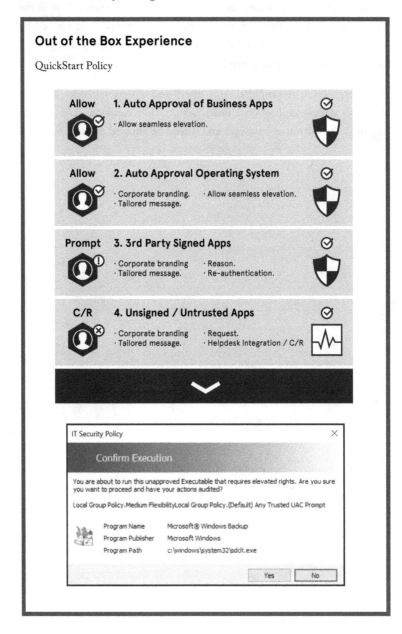

Utilising a set of business logic rules to build a baseline policy is one of the most effective and quickest to deploy methods, even within the largest of organisations. Business logic is built into each rule to capture applications requiring elevation, prohibit untrusted applications and protect trusted applications from malicious content. To achieve the above, you will need to select a solution with an extensive set of application definition criteria and very flexible rule logic.

The DiD approach described in this book makes this possible. Firstly, you have removed administrative accounts, and as a result, you can trust key areas for the build, allow applications to run from these locations and prohibit applications running from untrusted locations. This allows application whitelisting to be implemented.

The second step is to incorporate business logic into the rule set that detects applications, tasks, scripts and installers requiring administrative privileges (triggering UAC) and challenge the user to justify why they need to run them with administrator privileges. Logic can be incorporated to allow benign operating system functions to be elevated by the users, whilst prohibiting them from elevating potentially dangerous or malicious applications. The user can be shown a number of different messaging options to ask for justification, re-authentication or unlock codes (I will cover these in more detail later).

Finally, untrusted content from external sources will be prevented from attacking trusted applications. This approach is ideal for organisations that have migrated away for XP or Server 2003. The key reason for this is that UAC can be leveraged to detect when an application requires administrative privileges.

## Rule logic

I have provided a worked example below of how I typically set up rules to accommodate this approach. Obviously, every vendor's solution works differently; therefore, I have kept the example simple to illustrate the point. One thing to note is this approach assumes rules are processed in a top-down order.

Later in this section, I have included some use cases that must be accommodated for in your baseline policy design. I would typically design three levels of flexibility in the baseline policy (High/Medium/Low) to allow a broad range of user experiences; I will discuss this in more detail later in this section.

| # | Rule Name | Matching Criteria | Description |
|---|-----------|-------------------|-------------|
| 1 | Pro Auto Approved business apps file | programfiles% +Trusted Owner +UAC | Applications installed in the protected program files location will be allowed to run. They will also be elevated if needed |
| 2 | Trusted App Protection | %programfiles% +ParentPorcess +ChildProcess | Trusted applications which try to run child processes outside of their installation binaries will be blocked. |
| 3 | Auto Approved OS Functions | systemroot% +UAC | Applications which are digitally signed by a trusted vendor will be allowed to run. Any requesting admin privileges will receive gated access. |

DEFENCE IN DEPTH IS GREAT IN THEORY – BUT HOW DO I IMPLEMENT IT?

231

| 4 | 3rd Party signed applications | userprofile% +PublishCert | Applications which are digitally signed by a trusted vendor will be allowed to run. Any requesting admin privileges will receive gated access. |
| 5 | Unsigned & Untrusted applications | %userprofile% | Applications running from the user's profile will be prohibited from running, and the user will be asked for justification (see exception handling for more information) |

**Note: When deploying to macOSs you will need to include trusted locations; /System /Applications and protect untrusted locations /Users.**

### Baseline Use Cases – common scenarios

When building your baseline policy, the solution you select will need the following capabilities. Obviously, these will need to be included in your baseline policy design to provide a flexible experience. Design a policy which deals with each of these scenarios.

**Important: It only takes one use case that can't be achieved to grant admin privileges back to the user.**

## Application elevation

The solution should remove the reliance on local administrator accounts for the execution of applications that require elevated privileges. Instead, the product must be able to create access tokens with the correct set of privileges for the application to function. The solution must be able to detect the privileges required and generate the tokens dynamically.

### Common Privileged Tasks – Technical Users

- Windows Service configuration and control
- Native Application debugging (including performance profiling)
- Web application debugging (due to applications running in different user contexts)
- Building solutions (i.e. custom build steps including component registrations)
- Software Configuration (e.g. Visual Studio add-ins, COM toolbox controls)
- Configuration File Management (e.g. hosts file, application configuration files)

### Privileged Tasks – Mobile workers

- Installation of printer drivers and related management software
- Configuration of network settings (i.e. IP address and DNS settings)
- Installation and Management of external devices (e.g. 3G dongles, USB to RS232 adapters)

### Privileged Tasks – Universal Requirements

- Execution of Line of Business applications (e.g. MYOB)
- Self-service or centralised software deployment (e.g. SCCM appstore, installs in user context)

- Software installation and uninstallation
- Software update through inbuilt update mechanisms or patch installation
- System management and configuration (both desktop and server)
- Troubleshooting – Windows Service restarts (e.g. spooler or third party VPN services)

- Troubleshooting – System management (e.g. ipconfig /release or / flushdns, RSOP, gpresult)

## Application control

Application control (specifically whitelisting) is recognised as one of the most effective ways of securing an OS build, by preventing unknown applications from executing. This area of the product must be able to "trust" areas of the build and support features such as "trusted owner" (as described in chapter 5). The combination of location and trusted owner allows 80 to 90 per cent of line of business applications to be approved in one rule (see rule one in the above example). When combined with a privilege management solution that provides the flexibility of "on-demand" elevation, application control can provide all the benefits of a full whitelisting solution, without the administrative overheads.

### Unprivileged tasks and applications

Unprivileged tasks and applications can be equally problematic for organisations where there may be mixed requirements to permit, block or control these types of activities based upon the users' role requirements.

- Access to native system tools (e.g. PowerShell)
- Installation of user-space (i.e. user profile) applications
- Execution of standalone applications (i.e. portable applications)
- Visibility of the presence and usage of portable applications

- Access to, and use of, vulnerable third party applications (e.g. Java)
- Use of license controlled applications (both user installed and on shared environments)

## Application blacklisting

For restricted or unauthorised tasks, including a rule to explicitly block applications or scripts from execution is recommended. If the solution you choose has advanced matching criteria, applications can be blocked using any combination of rules or classifications - such as trusted ownership - or by tracking the origin of where an application was downloaded from. Without advance matching criteria this will not be feasible.

## Protection of trusted applications

Trusted line of business applications need to be protected from malicious content trying to exploit them, for example, a Word document being tricked into launching a fileless PowerShell exploit. There is no need for Word to be allowed to launch PowerShell, so by combining parent and child process matching criteria, these types of activity can be prohibited. If the solution you choose does not have the ability to determine execution privileges based on the parent process launching it, you will not be able to achieve this.

## User Account Control (UAC) replacement

User Account Control is designed to provide a confirmation prompt before a process can use administrator privileges. These prompts are often confusing for end users and can lead to increased demand on helpdesk teams to service their requests. The solution should allow an organisation to harness the UAC trigger and replace standard messages with customised messages that can be configured to block, elevate or audit activity. Complete customisation is required for the content and branding, this provides enhanced communication potential and improves end user experience.

## On-demand privilege elevation

Through integration into the Windows shell menu, the solution should replace the "Run as Administrator" option, providing specific users with the ability to elevate their privileges using an appropriate approval method. This ensures users can gain the access they need for one-off requests, without ever exposing the administrator account or password. Audits and reports on activity provide reports to monitor use.

## Challenge and response

For scenarios which are unclear, challenge and response is a great way to scrutinise the request. This feature typically provides the user with a single use 'challenge' code that requires a matching 'response' approval code. Once the user has the response code from the approver (typically the helpdesk), they are granted access to the application in an audited and controlled manner, even in areas without network connectivity. Look for functionality that can approve activity for single use, for the remainder of the session, or can be approved on a permanent basis.

Think about combining multiple authentication methods to create a dual authentication process, adding additional security layers to meet compliance requirements.

## COM elevation

The baseline policy will need to control operating system functions that are deeply embedded within the OS. There are over 300 OS functions that require COM elevation. The policy will need to replace all unwanted prompts with customisable behaviour; rule 3 is an example of this. Without this feature, tasks such as managing network and advanced network settings or changing firewall settings would require an administrator account.

## URL filtering

The solution should track all downloaded applications with the origin URL. These tracked downloads can then be enforced in policy to ensure that only applications from approved or reputable sources are allowed to execute – with all untrustworthy downloads being blocked and audited.

I would typically combine this feature with other capabilities such as UAC interception; this then becomes an immensely powerful way of identifying good and bad application executions.

## Tamper protection

Look for a solution that has built-in anti-tamper features, which prevent any changes to local privilege groups (including the administrator account/group) to stop any user from elevating their privileges. Users are also prevented from changing or altering the solution technology, ensuring the deployment is protected. Additionally, ensure tokens are protected from code injection, token hi-jack and shatter attacks. Otherwise, you will be implementing something less secure than the operating system.

## Service control

One of the most common administrative tasks performed on servers is the stopping and starting of services. The feature should allow individual service operations to be whitelisted, so that standard users can start, stop and configure services without the need to elevate tools, such as the Service Control Manager.

No modifications should be made to any service's discretionary access control list (DACL), keeping the security and integrity of the server build intact. I've seen many solutions which weaken the configuration settings to achieve this rather than dynamically elevating the request. Applying the baseline policy to servers will require this functionality. Try to combine criteria like "digital certificates", thus giving you the ability to allow all services from a particular vendor to be changed.

## Remote PowerShell management

A great way to make configuration changes to multiple servers (or any endpoint) is via PowerShell. When managing servers, you will need the ability to allow these connections and elevate them, as this functionality requires administrator privileges. I would typically include this functionality in my High flexibility policies (discussed later). This would allow the user to execute PowerShell scripts or cmdlets that are elevated, blocked or audit. This removes the requirement for users to create a terminal connection on a remote machine, which exposes more functionality that may be required to complete the task.

## Delegated Run As

This type of capability provides a targeted, policy controlled alternative to Windows Run As, whereby applications and tasks may be executed in the context of a secondary account. The applications where Delegated Run As can be used, by whom, and also the accounts or group of accounts that can be used, are all predetermined by the solution policies. This is a great support desk use case; the support operative would remote onto a user's endpoint and approve the activity. I typically include this for improved exception handling.

## Patch management/control

Utilising features such as on-demand privilege elevation and challenge and response, you can allow patches and updates to be applied without having to add them to a fixed policy, and importantly, without providing an administrator account. If you have configured flexible on-demand and challenge and response rules, nothing should be required to make this work.

## Licence control

When used in conjunction with an application control policy, it is possible to eliminate the installation and execution of unlicensed applications, providing a cost-effective method of controlling or even reducing licence budgets, and ensuring you remain compliant with licence mandates. Again, if application control is configured correctly, this will just work.

## Application definition criteria

Crucial to the success of any policy is the ability to combine application definition criteria together. You will need the following matching criteria to have any chance of achieving the approaches describing in this book. Cheaper solutions often cut corners and only offer basic non-configurable versions of these.

1. Filename
2. Command line
3. File Hash
4. Product Name
5. Publisher (certificate)
6. ActiveX Codebase
7. COM Class ID
8. App ID
9. Product Description
10. Product Version
11. File version

12. ActiveX Version

13. Product Code (installers)

14. Upgrade Code (installers)

15. Trusted Ownership

16. Requires Elevation (UAC)

17. Windows Store Package Name

18. Parent Process

19. Child Process

20. Windows Store Publisher

21. Windows Store Application Version

22. Source URL (web downloads)

You will need the ability to leverage wildcards and regular expressions to specify multiple application binaries with one rule while maintaining the level of specificity you require.

Additionally, you will need the ability to control the privileges assigned to individual child processes, or based on the parent process. These allow your organisation to create simple rules which are secure and flexible at the same time.

## Multiple streams of flexibility (High/Medium/Low)

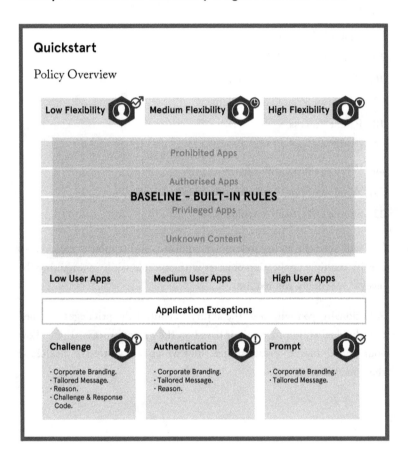

It is unrealistic to think a single baseline policy can be created to accommodate all of your end user requirements. A flexible policy design platform is required, whereby different user profiles/policies can be created to match the varying needs of the different groups of users, e.g. task-based workers, mobile workers, power users. Policies and their rules can be stacked/ordered so that resultant sets of policies apply varying levels of controls to different policies. Applications can then be grouped together based on different user demands, further simplifying policy design.

I have found that creating three layered policies (High, Medium and Low) works for the vast majority of deployments. The rationale behind these are described below:

## High Flexibility

This policy is designed to be provided to users who would need a lot of autonomy over their endpoint and would be very difficult to restrict, for example developers, engineers etc. This group of users is often referred to as innovators. When exceptions are raised, the user is asked to self-approve the action, the data will then be recorded.

## Medium Flexibility

This policy is designed to be provided to users who would occasionally install new applications, but when they do, they must justify their actions with a reason why. Employees such as tele-workers and marketers may fall into this category. These users are often referred to as 'knowledge' workers. Exceptions may trigger gated access or self-approval based on the severity of the action.

## Low Flexibility (Corporate Baseline)

This policy should be provided to users who would never need to install or make any changes to their endpoint themselves, such as kiosk and sales workers. Any such changes should be managed through a central service desk. This group are often referred to as 'process' workers. All exceptions are gated and audited.

I recommend deploying this policy to everyone in the environment and treating this policy as your corporate baseline. The advantage to this is that it should include exception handling capabilities (explained later) that deal with one-off requests these users may have. It should also add application whitelist controls to protect against ransomware and protect trusted applications.

## Layered policy design

Policy layering enables you to dramatically reduce the Total Cost of Ownership (TCO) of the solution and ensures that your build remains clean, simple and scalable. Utilising the solution across all endpoints, organisations are able to create rules for all user profiles within the environment. Once logged in with standard user accounts, the policy applied will provide the level of flexibility required based on the user's roles and requirements.

Typically, policies will also offer levels of flexibility based on job description or seniority, where process workers and external contractors are given tighter, more regulated restrictions than more senior roles.

The key here is that the policies will be aggregated together, building on the previous layer. For example, the high flex policy will include functionality in the medium and low. Most users will fall into the 'knowledge' and 'innovators' categories, which will build on top of the process worker's policy.

## Don't ask users what they need

I am not suggesting user communities should not be consulted; of course, they should. However, if you ask them a direct question about what access they need, the answer you get back will be 'full access' (in other words administrative privileges). It is extremely unlikely they will deliver a set of clearly defined use cases.

I would recommend you start by defining a list of job roles or policies. These will range from process worker to innovators. This will give you a good starting point to establish the types of use case they will need.

**The list below indicates typical use cases that a technical user might require:**

- Installing software
- Installing device drivers
- Changing Windows OS settings
- Manually installing updates

Once the user profiles are defined, I recommend mapping them across to one of the three policies.

## Advanced policy filtering

The solution you choose should accommodate filters to assign policies to the right user at the right time. Filters should include; security group membership, machine or hostname, time of day/ week, and expiry date/ time. It must be possible to in combine these together.

Many of the premium products even support filters which identify Microsoft Remote Desktop Services and Citrix XenApp remote connections, allowing policies to be targeted at remote sessions based on the hostname or IP Address of the remote user. Privileges can then be assigned only to approved remote clients, or through specific routed IP ranges.

A powerful WMI and PowerShell filtering engine allows policies to be targeted at specific infrastructures using any combination of the thousands of properties. For example, policies granting privileged access to IIS administration tools can be targeted at servers with the IIS role installed.

 **Look for a solution with a wide range of filtering options available. This will help ensure individuals or teams can be managed based on role, job function or even specific tasks, rather than as a one-size-fits-all.**

## Exception Handling

**Exception handling**

- Automatic suppression of UAC and seamless elevation
- Seamless sandboxing of untrusted sites and content
- Comprehensive end user messaging to handle Exceptions
  - > Corporate branding
  - > Full text configuration and localization
  - > Reason/request entry
  - > Helpdesk Integration (hyperlink or email)
  - > Password and smartcard authentication
  - > Challenge/response mechanism
  - > Over the shoulder administration

The next challenge is all about how you deal with exceptions. Exception handling options are required to ensure that applications, operating system functions, tasks, scripts and installations are only restricted for valid reasons. Anyone having a valid business reason to use/install a restricted item will have the option of requesting access when prompted. This can be achieved by implementing challenge and response functionality, whereby a request is sent to the IT helpdesk for a secure code to gain the access they need. This is all within the context of a standard user account.

Look for solutions that allow this to be automated with ticketing systems, and email/web alerts, as well as customised with corporate branding and text. This ensures a rich and intuitive user experience, without heavy resource requirements.

> **The key is not to get in the way of the user's ability to do his/her job. Choose the solution that provides the most comprehensive set of exception handling options.**

As discussed, scenarios will arise where exceptions need to be made and users are able to request access to functionality outside of their defined policy, e.g. a mobile worker needs to install software off-site. Exception handling ensures you have a strategy for dealing with these grey areas and is key to ensuring the balance between security and user freedom, by providing users with the options to easily request access to any unknown applications. This provides IT and security teams with the control and visibility they need to ensure security, while empowering users to be productive in their day-to-day job roles.

In my experience, well-developed policies should be able to deal with 80 to 85 per cent of cases the user encounters. The remaining 15 to 20 per cent will be dealt with via exception handling, and therefore this plays a crucial role in the success of your project.

**Below are the most common exceptions handling options I've come across:**

- **Challenge and response.** A customisable message will be displayed providing a challenge code for which a response code is needed to proceed. The response code can be communicated to the user by text message, URL or by helpdesk integration. The system should ask a series of questions before granting the response code to ensure the user needs the application for a valid business purpose.

- **Ticketing request.** Following a customisable message or application launch, a helpdesk ticket could be automatically logged. Look for solutions that include a powerful and flexible scripting engine, which has been designed to allow integration into an organisation's existing infrastructure.

- **Email request.** A customisable message is displayed which prompts the user for information, which is then submitted by email to the responsible IT team/manager.

- **URL request.** A customisable message will be displayed that directs the user to a URL requesting information, which can be submitted to the responsible IT team/manager.

DEFENCE IN DEPTH IS GREAT IN THEORY – BUT HOW DO I IMPLEMENT IT?

247

- **Support authorisation.** A customisable message is displayed that requires an authorised user to type in their credentials to proceed.

## Discovery mode (aka silent monitoring)

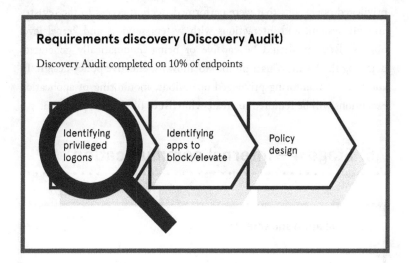

An alternative to using business logic is to monitor silently. I've included this here for completeness, although is it rarely used on modern operating systems. It was the default approach of pre-Windows Vista and Server 2008 operating systems.

To do this, you will need a solution that has the capability to be deployed in 'discovery mode', allowing privileged operations and privileged users to be monitored. This should also extend to application launches to establish prohibited applications.

Another key requirement here is the ability to analyse the data discovered. Look for a solution that has enterprise-class data analysis allowing this information to be reviewed and categorised. The information gathered during this stage will be used to provide context to the monitoring data and influence policy design.

The privilege monitoring reports should be detailed, and not only list the applications and privileges they require, but also include the actual privileged operations that were performed, such as access to the registry and file system, and interactions with system services and kernel level objects. Reports should be capable of being automatically generated, detailing the business' user profiles to allow for effective policy design. In addition to monitoring privileged operations, monitoring of application executions will be required to create whitelist or blacklist applications.

## 7.5. **Stage 4 – Internal communication**

**Internal announcements**

Internal comms templates provided based on our past experience

We will advise on a best practice approach to manage change

Users positively accept change if well communicated

T-minus style communications keep users updated

The political and cultural challenges of implementing DiD can be hard to overcome if not tackled in the correct way. I cannot stress enough how important this stage is to the success of your project. If not done effectively, this and this alone could be the downfall of the project. Consequently, I place a significant emphasis on user education and communication.

It is expected that users will accept change if it is communicated well, allowing them to understand the benefits. This will help minimise helpdesk support incidents related to the removal of elevated accounts. It's also important to set up a feedback mechanism (e.g. intranet, email, nominated contact) for questions and answers. It is very important to communicate the change prior to rollout.

 **Although this is the first time I have talked about end-user communication in detail, it is important to note that there may be multiple communication stages within a project, and so I recommend reviewing where in the project plan this should fit and choose the optimal place for your environment.**

## User push back

You should be prepared for users to push back once administrative accounts are removed and application control is put in place. In addition, do not be surprised if you lose the backing of management when faced with an unhappy workforce. I have seen so many security projects fail when security gets in the way of a user's ability to do their job. Users may feel that such measures are draconian and that they are not trusted.

The larger the organisation, the more likely such projects will be supported and seen as normal, and I would expect less push back.

## User acceptance – security should be seen as an enabler

Crucially, user acceptance comes down to presenting the changes in a positive light. Users are more likely to accept change if they understand it and feel they are gaining. Security should be an enabler. It is important to make sure you not only communicate how their computing experience will change and improve, but also explain the benefits for the company.

 I have seen projects fail when they have not been communicated effectively and the policy design has been dictated to end users. In fact, I've seen the solution deployed to 10,000 machines WITHOUT any policy testing, and this ultimately failed, as the DiD policies could not provide the correct level of elevation.

A well-designed DiD strategy allows users to fulfil their responsibilities without being exposed to unnecessary risks and maintains performance and reliability. Information and systems security is in the interest of the company, ensuring it can remain competitive.

## DiD is for everyone – that includes executives

I have discussed the importance of management buy-in already, but it is also important that managers set an example and are part of the project themselves. Too often, managers decide to exclude themselves, solely on the basis that they are a part of management. However, if managers don't think a scheme is important, neither will the employees.

## Language can be your downfall

The language used to promote the project should be positive, and it is best to avoid using language such as 'lockdown' and 'restricted privileges'. Such terms do not sit well with users and create the feeling that draconian controls are being put in place. If users can no longer perform a particular task on their endpoint, be ready to provide some justification.

## End users are not idiots

Explain the WHY! Users will be more receptive to the project if they understand why you are implementing DiD. Explain the thought processes and how the decisions have been made. Mentioning the security aspects directly should be avoided. Failure to communicate creates an environment of suspicion and control. It is important that users understand why IT is trying to secure the environment and how this will help their job roles.

 I have worked with an engineering organisation which had all the right intentions but failed to communicate with the end users and gather requirements. Instead, they imposed policy on them. In addition, there was no feedback mechanism. This ultimately led to failure.

### Security Workshops

Education will establish trust and get users on-side. Done right, users will be more aware of why security initiatives are important, how they are relevant to their own roles, and how security issues affect the business' profit if security workshops are run.

## 7.6. Stage 5 – Baseline testing and deployment

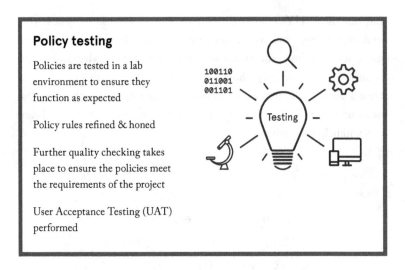

**Policy testing**

Policies are tested in a lab environment to ensure they function as expected

Policy rules refined & honed

Further quality checking takes place to ensure the policies meet the requirements of the project

User Acceptance Testing (UAT) performed

It is of the utmost importance that the recommended policy design is ratified by your organisation, tested and then rolled out in phases (starting small and increasing once User Acceptance Testing (UAT) results are positive). Regardless of the size of your enterprise, you should start small. I have worked with some of the largest organisations on the planet and had to reset expectations on the testing sizes, so be prepared to go smaller than you'd expect.

## Pilot

The implementation of DiD within your organisation should begin with a pilot, which must consist of users from different business units. If your organisation is standardised on a single OS, has little to no variance in configuration, and has a very controlled and predictable environment, a pilot may not be necessary. However, most organisations will perform some sort of pilot, and this should align to project goals and objectives to ensure they are met.

 **WORKSHEET**

| Items to validate during the pilot | |
| --- | --- |
| Technical and operational infrastructure integration | |
| How to roll-out the software to endpoints | |
| Refine project requirements | |
| Establish how best to communicate with end users | |
| Refine the goals and objectives | |
| Establish how to communicate the outcome to users and management | |
| Installation - time and complexity | |
| Usage - ease of use, completeness of solution in regards to requirements | |
| Overall experience, product and vendor | |

| | |
|---|---|
| Establish rule review criteria, process and responsibilities that mimic actual teams involved in day-to-day operations. | |
| End users must have communication validation | |
| Determine integration with existing change control procedures and policies. | |
| Determine the team responsible for implementation and ongoing support. | |
| Establish procedures for coordinating efforts between team members. | |
| Validate that the test environment is fully functional | |
| Test users from multiple groups within the organisation | |
| Aim to test 40% to 60% of use cases built into policies | |
| Perform co-exist testing | |
| Run User Acceptance Testing feedback sessions, which will lead to policy tweaking | |

The users selected for the pilot will have the solution deployed to their machines in order to ensure the correct balance has been struck between security and freedom. This will involve the removal of local administrative accounts and the addition of Application Control. Each user in the pilot group should work as normal to ensure that all approved and necessary applications and processes are working properly.

It is recommended that all test users are allowed to work for at least a few days to ensure that all normal day-to-day applications and processes have been identified. Any instances where users experience problems can be addressed quickly and policies adjusted accordingly.

The size and duration of the pilot will need to be determined by the project team and should align with your organisation's process and procedures. The pilot should not be longer than it needs to be, but must be long enough to allow issues to be established. The pilot must demonstrate how the solution can be used to improve the security posture and operational efficiencies within an environment.

**I would recommend running a pilot that looks like the following:**

- Has multiple departments
- Includes custom or industry applications
- Supports multiple versions of Windows desktops and servers
- Large help desks to support a diverse environment

## Product deployment

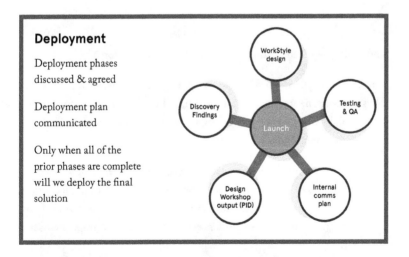

**Deployment**

Deployment phases discussed & agreed

Deployment plan communicated

Only when all of the prior phases are complete will we deploy the final solution

WorkStyle design

Testing & QA

Internal comms plan

Design Workshop output (PID)

Discovery Findings

Launch

Although we have covered a lot of ground at this point in the project, we still have a lot of decisions to make. For example, deployment phases, UAT period and rollout plans all need to be considered. Now the pilot is complete; the remaining corporate user base will be ready for deployment. This will be a phased rollout, with the phases based around:

- Site
- Department/business unit
- Geographical location
- User role
- Asset type
- Network architecture considerations
- Your business needs and implementation plan
- OS versions

Consideration must be given to the existing architecture of the endpoints and the overall network. I would recommend grouping similar assets (desktops and servers) and locations together, as this will ensure the experiences are similar and you are not dealing with multiple problems should they arise.

Also, consider future OS changes and the overall technology. Do the OS and policies applied need to be altered due to OS version?

Think about geographical location. If engineering is located in every physical building and location, including all engineering desktops in one phase might not be the ideal solution. Instead, organising the desktops per location or city might be a better approach.

I would recommend looking for existing deployment methodologies within your organisation and aligning to those. For example, logical groupings may align with existing Active Directory Organisation Units (OU) and may be the best guidance for managing the implementation by group.

## Planning

Planning and execution is the key to a successful implementation. Analysis of the pilot results will feed into the production rollout plan and help the refinement of goals and objectives. This will allow the production release plan to be updated easily. If the pilot has flagged up issues with either the technology or the planning, you need to review the approach for production implementation. The following are examples of areas that can cause problems and ultimately delay the deployment process:

• No clearly defined success criteria

• Unrealistic schedule for deployment (i.e. rushed rollout)

• Lack of commitment or user involvement from the defined functional groups

• Changes in the project leadership before completion

• Production system images and applications not included in the pilot group

• Exceptions handling is not correctly set up

During the pilot it is extremely important to document any challenges that occurred and the resolutions. These could be related to a number of areas, including technology, internal change control procedures and support staff requirements. Use this information to refine the remaining project stages as the solution is deployed across the enterprise. These may result in some stages being replayed, such as the policy design stages. This will diminish over time.

## Deployment Schedule

| Week | Task |
| --- | --- |
| 1 | Deploy the policy to 50 machines and gather feedback. |
| 2 | Meet to discuss feedback and make any tweaks/changes required, re-test. |
| 3 | Increase the coverage of the policy to 100 machines. |
| 4 | Meet to discuss feedback and make any tweaks/changes required-test. |
| 5 | Increase the coverage of the policy to 200 machines. |
| 6 | Meet to discuss feedback and make any tweaks/changes required, re-test. |
| 7-X | Keep doubling deployment numbers and tweaking until your reach 1,000 machines. |
| 8 | It is common at this point to factor some time in here for knowledge transfer and possible helpdesk training. |
| 9 | In larger environments, it is recommended to run the solution over a number of weeks, increasing the coverage of the policy so that one global site gets complete coverage. In this case, I would normally recommend that this site be one that is geographically close to (in the same time zone as) the main point of contacts for the support of the solution. |
| 10 | Once 1,000 machines have been reached, the rollout starts to hit larger quantities as most of the tweak will have been made. Continue to increase the policy to cover extra business units/global sites until we have reached all machines/users in scope for the production policy. |

Once 1,000 endpoints have been deployed, it is common to make big leaps in the deployment numbers, as most of the kinks have been worked out.

## Removing administrator accounts

There are many ways to remove administrative accounts; typically, I recommend one of the following:

- **Restricted Users and Groups GPO:** This can be used to wipe and reapply group settings or append.

- **Local Users and Groups Extension (Preferences):** Group Policy includes the Local Users and Groups preference extension. This extension allows you to manage local users and groups on domain member computers centrally.

Other common methods include startup scripts and SCCM configuration tasks. I would recommend performing some research and testing these out in a lab environment prior to production rollout. It is also important to understand how rights are granted in the first place. I have seen organisations remove administrative accounts, only to find higher precedence GPOs reapply them.

With the two-wave approach I'm advocating here, admin accounts are removed much sooner than they would with a "Discovery Mode" approach. They can be removed as soon as the baseline policy is deployed.

When I delivered 100k seats to a defence contractor in the US, we aligned the provisioning of policy with the expiry of the existing admin account process. Users had to request administrative accounts periodically, and on expiry, they would be provisioned into the correct policy group within AD. This simplified the process and allowed for touch points with the end users.

Wave one is now complete.

## 7.7. Wave two - Stage 6 - User behavioural data review

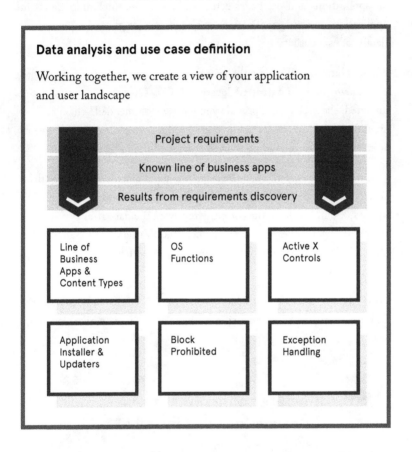

**Data analysis and use case definition**

Working together, we create a view of your application and user landscape

Project requirements

Known line of business apps

Results from requirements discovery

| Line of Business Apps & Content Types | OS Functions | Active X Controls |
| Application Installer & Updaters | Block Prohibited | Exception Handling |

Once the baseline policy has been in operation for some weeks/months, the data captured on actual user behaviour can be reviewed. It is therefore of the utmost importance that the report system provided by your tools produces meaningful data (see chapter 5 for examples of the types of data you will need).

Reporting dashboards should leverage the power of databases technologies such as SQL to provide a breakdown of all user and application privileges. This data can be used to gain a holistic view of all applications and privileges across the enterprise, including trends in application demand, applications executed outside the core policy and details of user activity.

Many solutions will review the privileged operations in conjunction with the known apps and trusted locations/rules. Once the data has been analysed, the tool should provide you with "recommended" changes. You should also be able to see if any users need downgrading (moved to low from medium) or upgrading (moved from medium to high).

I previously deployed 55,000 endpoints to a global consulting firm, which initially placed 14,000 users in high flex, 13,000 in medium flex and 28,000 in low flex. The company reviewed the data after two months of use and were able to move a further 10,000 users (who claimed that they needed an administrator account) to low flex and only had to upgrade 500 users.

Any changes must be ratified by someone who fully understands the business need, rather than being entirely automated, which can often lead to policy misconfiguration.

 **The tooling you select should be capable of incorporating your business logic. For example, if you install all of your business applications to C:\program files\mycompany and an application which runs from here triggers administrative accounts to be utilised, then we can assume this is a valid line of business application.**

## 7.8. **Stage 7 – Policy refinement/additional policy design**

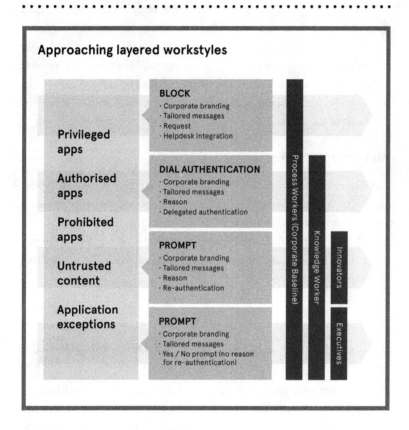

**Approaching layered workstyles**

Privileged apps

**BLOCK**
· Corporate branding
· Tailored messages
· Request
· Helpdesk integration

Authorised apps

**DIAL AUTHENTICATION**
· Corporate branding
· Tailored messages
· Reason
· Delegated authentication

Prohibited apps

Untrusted content

**PROMPT**
· Corporate branding
· Tailored messages
· Reason
· Re-authentication

Application exceptions

**PROMPT**
· Corporate branding
· Tailored messages
· Yes / No prompt (no reason for re-authentication)

Process Workers (Corporate Baseline)

Knowledge Worker

Innovators

Executives

The work carried out in stage 6 will allow you to establish your policy design changes. In my experience, it's typical this stage will produce two more policies which sit between low-medium and medium-high. It is unusual for more than five policies to be required. The most I have ever seen across the nine million endpoints I've been involved with is ten. The same design principle outlined in stage 3 should be adhered to when creating additional policies.

## Workflow automation

Now is a good time to consider automation of workflows, such as automatically logging helpdesk tickets for exceptions or for blocked applications. Look for a solution that can leverage extensible integration capabilities, i.e. the ability to execute custom scripts before and after execution. A solution that is capable of triggering a script can provide instant feedback into existing workflow or management systems. The more of the management system that can be automated, the lower the total cost of the ownership.

## Management automation

The larger the environment, the less likely you are to want to spend time administrating the solution. It is therefore essential to choose a solution that can fully automate policy changes. This allows system administrators to create and modify the solution's policies directly through external workflow management solutions. Check that the automation capabilities are comprehensive and not just for a small number of capabilities.

# 7.9. **Stage 8 – Deployment of refined policies**

By this point, your deployment experiences gained from stage 5 will put you in an excellent position to deploy any changes and newly designed policies. Rather than repeat these recommendations, you can merely refer back to stage 5 for testing deployment recommendations.

## 7.10. Stage 9 - Business as usual support (Post deployment)

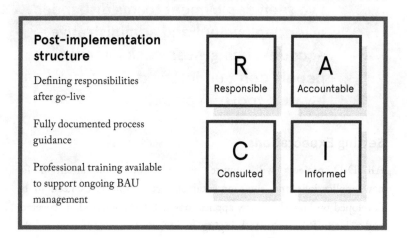

**Post-implementation structure**

Defining responsibilities after go-live

Fully documented process guidance

Professional training available to support ongoing BAU management

**R** Responsible

**A** Accountable

**C** Consulted

**I** Informed

After deployment, there is still work to be done, in the form of ensuring you have established post-deployment ownership. In my experience, many organisations often overlook the importance of deciding post-implementation project structure. However, it is important to ensure the areas of responsibilities are defined so that you have the structure in place to refine and adapt the policies to the needs of your organisation evolve. Once established, I would recommend setting up a business as usual handover procedure to ensure the teams that are managing the solution fully accept their areas of ownership. This should include product and process training.

 You need a product that will grow with you and not be restrictive.

I generally recommend my clients build a RACI (Responsible, Accountable, Consulted, Informed) matrix, as shown in the image

above. Although this is discussed at stage 9, this really should be built throughout the life of the project.

 **I've seen deployment teams disbanded after deployment and administrative accounts being given back because people don't understand or are not aware a tool is in place.**

### Setting Expectations

All DiD projects will require post-implementation attention for new applications and environmental changes. Procedures need to be developed on how these new applications will be monitored, discovered, and solved. This includes bringing in various teams to report on the change and implement the solution.

Expectations will need to be set to ensure users do not place unreasonable demands on the teams owning the solutions. Creating a catalogue of services that your IT department offers helps to set expectations. Service catalogues show the business how IT services align with business needs, establishing trust between IT and the business, by illustrating the value of services.

### Support service level agreements (SLAs)

Ensure you set both internal and external SLAs. Internal SLAs can be documented in the service catalogues. If the product vendor needs to be involved, ensure that the vendor has SLAs that meet your needs and is available when you need it. For example, is 24/7/365 support for all products and technologies included in the solution?

## Knowledge Transfer

It is impossible to expect the solution owners to get the best out of the solution if they have not had training. Team members need to be trained on the various aspects of the solution, including communication, training and labs for testing any in-project items. The solution and the different components also need to be documented. This would typically be built up through the life of the project and handed over at the end as an "as built" document.

**Typical items include:**

- Policy deployment architecture
- Reporting architecture
- Agent deployment architecture
- Delegation of control models used
- Policy and rule logical
- New policy, rule and definition creation

CHAPTER 8

# Building group consensus

By now you will be able to see how success can be achieved. However, before you start a project like this, there is one more challenge to overcome – group consensus. In the face of large and complex organisations, with multiple decision makers, this can be a challenge. I have seen many organisations settle for what is essentially weak security because they simply struggled to agree on anything else. Without consensus, the project may never see the light of day.

I have helped many business leaders and technical stakeholders navigate the process of consensus building, and that is what I want to focus on in this chapter. I have broken this process into four stages. The focus here is to help establish your business objectives and not to build a project delivery team (that is covered in chapter 7).

## 8.1. **Stage one – Understanding group conflict**

If one thing is certain, there will be group conflict. You should not shy away from this; instead confront this as early in the process as possible. Try to understand the viewpoints of all stakeholders and clearly document the issues facing them and their teams. Do not wait until later in the project in the hope that the issues will go away, as this approach runs a greater risk of completely derailing the project and resulting in failure.

Once you understand the pain points, bring suppliers in earlier than you would typically aim to. Studies have shown that group conflict peaks at 37 per cent, yet project stakeholders do not seek external advice until they are 57 per cent certain the project will work[1]. Think about this for a moment – how many projects have failed before they have even started?

## 8.2. **Stage two – Build the team**

Understand who the key decision makers are in the process and involve them from the start. Do not leave out potential road blockers (if they should be involved), as they will only put the project at risk after a large amount of effort has been put in. There are typically 5.4 decision makers[2] involved in enterprise projects and the more people involved; the less likely the project will be a success. However, do not be fooled into thinking people can be left out of the decision-making process. Not including them will only have detrimental effects further down the line.

---

1     The Challenger Customer by CEB
2     The Challenger Customer by CEB

The key here is to understand the traits of the individuals in the team. This will allow you to play to their strengths, whilst mitigating any issues they may cause. Look for people that exhibit the following traits:

- Champions good ideas
- Always delivers more than asked
- Learns from mistakes and does not repeat
- Often teaches insights to colleagues
- Colleagues and senior executives seek their advice
- Good at convincing others
- Perceives unclear projects as risky and wants to clarify
- Prepares influential stakeholders for disruptive ideas
- Believes changes require small wins first which build over time

My experience has shown that focusing on people that exhibit the above traits creates a recipe for success. Typically, you would not find someone that holds skills in all of the above areas, so try to bring a team together that blends the above.

## 8.3. Stage three – Confronting group conflict

Set up workshops to discover the pain points, business objectives, requirements and success criteria for the project. Look for consultants and vendors who can offer technology agnostic workshops, which can help you navigate the conflicts and come up with workable solutions. Search for insight into the scope of any consultancy effort, for both Proof of Concepts (PoCs) and production deployment.

If members of the team are prohibitive, try to break down their mental models that are stopping group consensus being agreed upon and address each issue head-on. Use the workshops for this and look for consultants and vendors to provide insight as to when and how they have solved these issues before. Avoid vendors who lack real-world experience or just tell you what you want to hear.

Focusing on the following areas early will help identify issues, without waiting until substantial work has been conducted. The aim of the workshop should be to identify and measure points of conflict. Encourage the exchange of views, especially if conflicting - this helps you break down objections should they arise. The list below will ultimately lead to clear project success criteria.

- Discuss priorities/needs and highlight differences
- Uncover subtle/unexpected implications
- Uncover unvoiced concerns
- Identify benefits of the right solution
- Identify consequences and costs of not acting
- Ask influencers to share why others are supporting the project
- Drive debate into the "too hard" or "too stressful" areas
- What do we not know but should?
- What are we missing?
- Focus on getting things right vs just getting things done

### ✏ WORKSHEET

| Prepare | |
|---|---|
| Clear purpose and agenda - and start on time | |

| Manage | |
|---|---|
| Restate purpose and agenda at the start | |
| Control interruptions | |
| Protect the shy and quiet (encourage their input) | |
| Contain the noisy (stop them dominating) | |
| Control discussions that wander off the point | |
| Stop "meetings within meetings" | |
| Accept differences of opinion – but contain conflict between individuals – keep to business issues | |
| Ensure everyone is involved and contributing | |
| Record points of view – I often use a flip chart for this – that way everyone can see the recorded items | |

| Close | |
|---|---|
| Call a halt: Remind everyone of goals and objectives | |
| Summarise input from all sides | |
| Agree next steps | |
| Finish on time | |
| Follow up | |
| Document outcome and actions asap and distribute | |

CHAPTER 9

# Tools and vendor selection

In this chapter, I set out key criteria which should be looked at when choosing a vendor. These do not only apply to DiD projects, but can generally be used for any IT projects. The order the criteria are presented here is important.

## 9.1. **Security**

Security needs to be built into the solution from the ground up and not retrofitted or applied over the top, as this will inherently lead to weakness in the solution and ultimately allow it to be bypassed. Consider the proposed solution against the following:

- **Protect the integrity of the solution:** The solution must be intelligent enough to protect itself, with in-built security measures. Users/malware must not be able to leverage elevated processes to disable or tamper with the components of the solution.
- **Local system protection:** The solution must prevent the manipulation of privileged user account groups.
- **Malware attack vector protection:** The solution must offer protection against common malware attack vectors, including code injections, shatter attacks and token hijacks.
- **Policy authenticity:** The solution should include the option for policies to be controlled, only allowing the right people to author and distribute.
- **Multi-layered management delegation:** The solution must provide a delegation management platform, therefore allowing disparate teams to manage key aspects of the solution.
- **Proactive prevention:** The solution must allow you to establish and define what trusted software within your environment is. This secures endpoints by preventing untrusted software, such as advanced and targeted threats, from executing in your environment.
- **Complements existing security solutions:** The solution should integrate with existing tools and not prohibit them from functioning.
- **Granular control of administrative rights:** The solution must be able to apply targeted administrative privileges without having to over-privilege applications and users.

## 9.2. **Features**

You should consider the future and what requirements your organisation will have 12 months into the deployment. I have seen organisations choose solutions based on price, only to find it could not cope with the additional demand placed on it further down the line. Remember it only takes one use case you cannot achieve to grant admin privileges back, so all of these features are hugely important.

- **Process elevation:** Ensure that administrative privileges can be assigned to individual applications, tasks and scripts without requiring the user to be granted full administrative accounts, along with the ability to create custom privilege tokens.

- **Diverse application support:** The solution must provide broad application support, including native support of hosted file types, such as Control Panel Applets (.cpl) and Microsoft Management Consoles (.msc).

- **Board application identification:** The solution must support a broad and varied range of application identification criteria that are consistent across the tooling and provide the ability to combine multiple criteria together.

- **Application whitelisting:** Prevent the execution of unauthorised applications through a combination of user-centric application whitelisting and blacklisting.

- **Zero Day protection:** Protect trusted applications (e.g. Office) from web-borne threats that gain access to the users' data.

- **Identify privilege requirements:** Detect and audit which users, applications, installers, tasks and scripts require administrative privileges.

- **Auditing and reporting:** Provide application trend analysis, including which applications are being run, by which user and on which machines.

- **Feature parity:** Provides feature parity across management platforms and Operating Systems (where applicable).

## 9.3. **Ease of use**

The solution should start simple and stay simple regardless of the size of the deployment. Rapid deployment capabilities are important; no organisation wants to take months and years to deploy the solution. The approaches described in this book deliver results in weeks, but to do that, you need the capabilities described below.

- **Rapid deployment capabilities:** Vendors should have built "out of the box" policies which "just work" based on their experiences. These will need to be flexible to deal with unknown scenarios.

- **Easy to implement and maintain:** Policy design should be consistent and clear throughout the solution.

- **Custom messaging:** Effective communication with users should be central to this solution. Communication via customisable, corporately branded, end-user messaging will replace confusing and unintuitive system messages and therefore ensure flexibility and successful user adoption.

- **Request workflow:** The solution should provide a mechanism to allow the user to gain access to applications after providing justification and optional re-authentication to ensure a positive user experience while supporting tracking and auditing requirements.

- **Fully replace User Account Control (UAC) messages:** By overriding UAC, users have a mechanism to request access, with clear and concise messages that result in a superior end-user experience.

- **Minimal user impact:** The solution should be hassle-free for the end user.

## 9.4. Architecture
• • • • • • • • • • • • • • • • • • • • • • • • • • • • • • • • • • • • • • • • • • •

The solution must provide flexible deployment options. There maybe many occasions where one deployment option does not allow you to reach every endpoint. You need multiple options to support every eventuality. There is no point deploying the solution to 70 per cent of your environment, only to be breached by the 30 per cent not protected.

- **Integration with existing technologies:** The solution must have an option to utilise existing technologies such as Active Directory, Azure AD, AWS, Intune or other third party platform.

- **Reporting platform:** The reporting capabilities must be able to consolidate audit data into the existing central server that can correlate events over time by leveraging existing technologies.

- **Single agent:** Maintaining a lightweight core image is important, and therefore all features of the solution must be controlled through a single client-side agent that does not have a material impact on the performance of the endpoints.

- **Single management console:** Ongoing maintenance should be performed from a single point of administration and must not place a significant strain on internal resources.

- **Centrally managed policy:** The solution must provide a central mechanism for policies to be deployed.

- **Policy automation:** The solution must provide the ability to automate the creation and deployment of policies, through technologies such as PowerShell.

- **Comprehensive platform coverage:** The solution must cover all platforms equally, providing feature parity regardless of OS version or deployment technology used.

- **Scalability:** The solution must be capable of scaling to support hundreds of thousands of endpoints.

## 9.5. **Support and Consulting**

- **Global support:** The vendor must provide a support operation that is available 24 hours a day, 365 days a year, with access to local engineers and online ticketing for raising and tracking support cases.
- **Net Promoter Score (NPS):** Look into the vendor's NPS score to see how they perform against industry averages.
- **Professional services:** The solution must be accompanied by a professional services consultancy to aid in design and implementation. This is crucial to ensure project success and will support the handover of the solution to business as usual (BAU) operations.
- **Implementation methodology:** There must be a proven and robust implementation methodology surrounding the solution, based upon successful project deployments. This enables you to maximise investment and ensure the software deployment meets the defined requirements.

## 9.6. **Innovation**

Any vendor can say they are innovators or are going to innovate, but you can only judge them on their past performance, and the proof is in the numbers. Look for a vendor that has consistently innovated and pushed the boundaries of what can be achieved. Compare feature release notes to see which vendors have brought features to the market first.

## 9.7. **Vendor selection questions**

I have put together a set of questions that will help you in the event your organisation has to build a tender:

### Architecture and management

1.  What infrastructure is required to support the management of the solution?
2.  What platforms are supported for the management components of the solution?
3.  Does the solution integrate with existing infrastructure? (AD, Azure etc.)
4.  Does the solution support offline users?
5.  Does the solution support integration into third party frameworks?
6.  Does the solution support delegated administration?
7.  Does the solution support computer and/or user configurations?
8.  Does the solution support layered policies?
9.  Does the solution provide the ability to see the resultant set of policy applied?
10. What automation options does your solution provide?

### Privilege Management

1.  Does the solution allow users to work under standard user accounts?
2.  Does the solution support the seamless elevation of individual applications?
3.  Does the solution support advanced users, who may need to elevate applications on demand?

4. What types of application can the solution manage?

5. Does the solution provide application templates for built-in operating system tasks and common third-party applications?

6. Can applications be grouped together to simplify management?

7. Can policies be created that different target users and/ or computers?

8. Can temporary policies be created with expiry times?

9. Does the solution include built-in security tokens to grant administrative accounts to users?

10. Does the solution allow granular security tokens to be defined?

11. Can the inheritance of privileges by child processes be controlled?

12. Does the solution secure file open save dialogs within elevated applications?

13. Does the solution support the discovery of privileged applications before administrative accounts are removed from users?

14. Can the solution suppress or replace all UAC consent dialogs?

15. Does your solution support the remote management of machines and servers?

16. How are you going to provide different day-to-day functions for different job roles?

17. How does your solution deal with application installs coming from external sources, such as the internet?

## End-user experience

1. Does the solution allow a custom message to be displayed before an application is launched or blocked?

2. Can multiple messages be defined?

3. Is the message text fully configurable? Is multi-lingual support included?

4. Can an optional reason/request be included in a custom message?

5. Can the user be forced to re-authenticate before launching an application?

6. Can the messages be branded, for instance with a corporate logo or banner?

7. How are you going to handle messaging within your multi-regional workforce?

8. What exception handling capabilities exist in your application to deal with applications not defined in policy?

## Application control

1. Does the solution provide application control capabilities?

2. Does the solution support blacklisting and whitelisting simultaneously?

3. Does the solution support exception handling from restricted and unknown applications?

4. What types of applications can be controlled?

5. Does the solution support granular control of child process for black or whitelisting?

6. How does the solution protect against zero-day vulnerabilities in known, trusted applications?

7. What trusted applications can be protected?

8. Does your solution provide DLL protection?

9. Can your solution protect against fileless malware?

## Agent

1. Does the solution require an agent to be installed on the endpoint?
2. What platforms are supported by the agent?
3. How is the agent packaged?
4. Is the agent upgradable?
5. How does the agent protect its integrity?
6. What performance impact does the agent have on the system?
7. Are policies cached and still applied when the endpoint is not connected to the corporate network?
8. How are cached policies secured?

## Security of solution

1. Does your solution protect the admin group from modification?
2. Does your solution prevent users overriding the system from an elevated process?
3. Does your solution identify privilege logons?
4. Can you prevent the execution of unwanted child processes from an elevated application?
5. Can you allow the installation of applications to be executed securely from a trusted source, such as a URL? (app store etc.)
6. Can your solution provide granular, secure control for services?
7. How does your solution protect the elevated application from malware attacks?

## Security of data in cloud platforms

1. Do you have processes and procedures around physical access to the servers that host client data?

2. How do you vet employees with access to client data?

3. Is the environment shared or true multi-tenant? If shared, is the data guaranteed to be secure from other organisations?

4. If another customer was to overuse the environment, could it impact my solution?

5. How is data secured during transmission from the client to the server environment?

6. Do you maintain full audit trails of access to the environment?

7. Which country is the data stored in? Do you guarantee it will never leave that country?

## Auditing and reporting

1. Are centralised reporting capabilities available with the solution?

2. What platforms are supported for reporting?

3. What preconfigured dashboards and reports are included?

4. Can custom reports be created?

5. What events are audited?

6. What information is audited in these events?

7. Is there granular control over the raising of events?

8. Does your solution identify the applications that require admin accounts or that you want to block?

9. Does your solution provide details of why an application needs administrative privileges to run?

10. What trend analysis does your solution provide?

11. How does the solution analyse and provide
    policy recommendations?

## Implementation and training

1. What is the largest implementation of your solution?

2. Can you describe the phases of a typical implementation?

3. Does your company offer an official training course? What about
   support and maintenance?

4. What are your standard hours of support?

5. Do you offer 24/7 support?

6. What are your support response times?

7. Do you provide a standard Service Level Agreement?

8. What methods are available for engaging with your
   support function?

9. Do you have an online knowledge base?

10. Can you provide insight into your support statistics and
    customer satisfaction?

11. What tools are provided to troubleshoot your solution?

12. Does your solution provide "out of the box" policies to speed
    up deployment?

CHAPTER 10
# Final thoughts

Securing your endpoints does not have to be hard, but I constantly see history repeating itself. The irony is you do not need to be a security expert to protect your environment: you just need to build your environment on solid foundations. There are so many misconceptions about effectiveness and so much hype; I can see why the same attack vectors are exploited.

However, because of the range of implications, cybersecurity cannot be left entirely to the IT and security teams. Ultimately, the board will be held accountable if a company falls victim to a cyber attack and in many cases, they may be held personally liable. Everyone, including the CEO, now needs to take ownership and accountability over the security of important information. It is a company problem. The consensus building points I discussed in chapter 8 will help you bring all this together.

Regardless of the hacker's motivation, the consequences are the same - lost business, damaged reputation and a wide variety of immediate and longer-term expenses. With the number of data breaches continuing to grow, businesses can no longer hope that any incidents will go unnoticed. Consumers, organisations and investors are more sensitive than ever about the safety of personal data, and it will take a huge amount of work for firms to regain trust in the wake of a breach. You only have to take a brief look at the media to find examples of security warnings being repeatedly ignored by all facets of the organisations, leading to one outcome - a breach.

Throughout this book, I have talked about how the balance can be struck between security and freedom by detailing best practices derived from years of experience in assisting thousands of customers across millions of endpoints. These have included best practices for designing, planning, implementation and the ongoing maintenance of a DiD project, which combines three key concepts; privilege management, application control, and trusted application protection. Additionally, I have provided the pros and cons for a number of technologies typically used to attempt to solve the challenges in the areas discussed here. This enables you to go into this project better informed and provides the security foundations from which your environment can be built.

Partner with a solutions provider that has experience in the space and which understands the right way and the wrong way to deploy DiD. When discussing your project with the vendor, ensure they are talking in terms of project success and not simply focusing on the solution. The vendor should place significant emphasis on the design and planning stages of implementation. Review implementation experience, reference calls and case studies to ascertain what their background is. The right solution is crucial, but you also need to be able to operationalise it, which is the difference between success and failure.

## Key takeaways

1. Join up the dots between teams to truly establish your need state.

2. The threat landscape changes continually, outpacing detection based solutions, so do not build your strategy on detection.

3. Proactive measures play a strong role in a cyber kill chain and are proven to work.

4. Defend against zero-day and advanced threats by not repeating the mistakes of the past.

5. Do not ignore end-user freedom. If security gets in the way of productivity, it will be weakened.

6. Exception handling must form a core part of your requirements, as you cannot predict the future.

7.  Do not settle for average security; use it as an enabler for end-user freedom.

8.  Start with the end in mind and fully understand your requirements prior to starting the project.

9.  Deal with conflict early in the project, or it will affect your success.

10. Ensure you involve all the stakeholders from the start.

11. Do not just buy software, buy success.

This leads me to the final thing to say; by following the advice in the book, you should be able to find the elusive balance between security and freedom, to find a productive solution that works for everyone in the organisation – good luck and thankyou!

Should you have questions or want to discuss the items discussed throughout this book, you can find me at:

- **Linkedin** https://uk.linkedin.com/in/andrewavanessian
- **Twitter** @AndyAvanessian
- **Email** andrew_avanessian@hotmail.com

## APPENDIX

### Defaut local groups in Microsoft

| Group | Description | Default user rights |
|-------|-------------|---------------------|
| Administrators | Members of this group have full control of the computer, and they can assign user rights and access control permissions to users as necessary. The Administrator account is a default member of this group. When a computer is joined to a domain, the Domain Admins group is added to this group automatically. Because this group has full control of the computer, use caution when you add users to it. | • Access this computer from the network<br>• Adjust memory quotas for a process<br>• Allow logon locally<br>• Allow logon through Remote Desktop Services<br>• Back up files and directories<br>• Bypass traverse checking<br>• Change the system time<br>• Change the time zone<br>• Create a page file<br>• Create global objects<br>• Create symbolic links<br>• Debug programs<br>• Force shutdown from a remote system<br>• Impersonate a client after authentication<br>• Increase scheduling priority<br>• Load and unload device drivers<br>• Log on as a batch job<br>• Manage auditing and security log<br>• Modify firmware environment variables<br>• Perform volume maintenance tasks<br>• Profile single process<br>• Profile system performance<br>• Remove computer from docking station<br>• Restore files and directories<br>• Shut down the system<br>• Take ownership of files or other objects |

| Back up Operators | Members of this group can back up and restore files on a computer, regardless of any permissions that protect those files. This is because the right to perform a back up takes precedence over all file permissions. Members of this group cannot change security settings. | • Access this computer from the network<br>• Allow logon locally<br>• Back up files and directories<br>• Bypass traverse checking<br>• Log on as a batch job<br>• Restore files and directories<br>• Shut down the system |
|---|---|---|
| Cryptographic Operators | Members of this group are authorised to perform cryptographic operations. | No default user rights |
| Distributed COM Users | Members of this group are allowed to start, activate, and use DCOM objects on a computer. | No default user rights |
| Guests | In a computer joined to the domain, members of this group have a temporary profile created at log on, and when the member logs off, the profile is deleted. Profiles in workgroup environments are not deleted. The Guest account (which is disabled by default) is also a default member of this group. | No default user rights |

| Guests (continued) | Members of this group will have a temporary profile created at log on, and when the member logs off, the profile will be deleted. The Guest account (which is disabled by default) is also a default member of this group. | No default user rights |
| --- | --- | --- |
| IIS_IUSRS | This is a built-in group that is used by Internet Information Services (IIS). | No default user rights |
| Network Configuration Operators | Members of this group can make changes to TCP/IP settings, and they can renew and release TCP/IP addresses. This group has no default members. | No default user rights |
| Performance Log Users | Members of this group can manage performance counters, logs, and alerts on a computer — both locally and from remote clients — without being a member of the Administrators group. | No default user rights |

| Performance Monitor Users | Members of this group can monitor performance counters on a computer — locally and from remote clients— without being a member of the Administrators group or the Performance Log Users groups | No default user rights |
|---|---|---|
| Power Users | By default, members of this group have no more user rights or permissions than a standard user account. The Power Users group in previous versions of Windows was designed to give users specific administrator rights and permissions to perform common system tasks. In this version of Windows, standard user accounts inherently have the ability to perform most common configuration tasks, such as changing time zones. | No default user rights |

| Power Users (continued) | For legacy applications that require the same Power User rights and permissions that were present in previous versions of Windows, administrators can apply a security template that enables the Power Users group to assume the same rights and permissions that were present in previous versions of Windows. | No default user rights |
|---|---|---|
| Remote Desktop Users | Members of this group can log on to the computer remotely. | Allow logon through Remote Desktop Services |
| Replicator | This group supports replication functions. The only member of the Replicator group should be a domain user account that is used to log on the Replicator services of a domain controller. Do not add user accounts of actual users to this group. | No default user rights |

| Users | Members of this group can perform common tasks, such as running applications, using local and network printers, and locking the computer.<br><br>Members of this group cannot share directories or create local printers. By default, the Domain Users, Authenticated Users, and Interactive groups are members of this group. Therefore, any user account that is created in the domain becomes a member of this group. | Access this computer from the network<br><br>Allow logon locally Bypass traverse checking Change the time zone<br><br>Increase a process working set<br><br>Remove the computer from a docking station<br><br>Shut down the system |
| --- | --- | --- |
| Offer Remote Assistance Helpers | Members of this group can offer Remote Assistance to the users of this computer. | No default user rights |

# INDEX

ISBN: 978-0-244-45688-7

www.ingramcontent.com/pod-product-compliance
Lightning Source LLC
Chambersburg PA
CBHW071104050326
40690CB00008B/1113